English Together

at classroom

우종현(Jonghyeon Woo)

○ 백석문화대학교 교수
○ 한국영어어문교육학회 이사(전)
○ 한국현대언어학회 이사(전)

English Together at classroom

© 우종현, 2022

1판 1쇄 인쇄__2022년 8월 21일
1판 1쇄 발행__2022년 8월 31일

지은이__우종현
펴낸이__이종엽
펴낸곳__글모아출판
　　　　등록__제324-2005-42호
공급처__(주)글로벌콘텐츠출판그룹
　　　　대표_홍정표 이사_김미미 편집_임세원 강민욱 백승민 문방희 권군오 기획·마케팅_이종훈 홍민지
　　　　주소__서울특별시 강동구 풍성로 87-6
　　　　전화__02) 488-3280 팩스__02) 488-3281
　　　　홈페이지__http://www.gcbook.co.kr
　　　　이메일__edit@gcbook.co.kr

값 14,000원
ISBN 978-89-94626-94-9 93740

English Together

at classroom

우종현 지음

글모아출판

머리말

이 책은 초급대학의 교실수업 활용을 위해 엮어졌다.

초급대학 학생들이 기본적으로 알아야 할 영어에 대해서 아홉 가지 주제를 선정하여 이에 대한 내용 읽기 및 단어를 중심으로 엮었으며, 일상회화를 위한 표현 연습도 하도록 했다. 또한 문장 이해를 돕는 기초적인 영어 문장 구조 및 활용을 위한 문법을 다루고 있다.

전체 내용을 2개 Part로 구분하였으며, Part1에서 Topic based vocabulary & Reading Comprehension and Listening comprehension & Picture based Writing 으로, Part 2에서는 Grammar로 구성되어 있다.

일상생활에서 기본적으로 알아야 할 단어를 주제별로 제시하여 생활 영어표현을 이해하고, 그림의 내용을 표현하는 쓰기 연습과 짧은 대화를 듣는 연습을 통해 기초적인 실용영어의 초석을 다지도록 했다. 또한 편안하게 영어 문장 구조에 대한 이해를 하도록 함으로써, 영어에 대한 불안감을 해소하도록 엮었다.

Contents

PART II

Part

I

Words, Reading, Writing, Listening

Lesson
1

Campus life

Main Words (Campus life)

register	department
mandatory,	financial
requirement	furnished
certificate	absent
dormitory	utility
library	cafeteria
semester	term
credit	degree
course	graduation
verification	academy

Fill in the blank with a suitable word

He _____ at Seoul College three weeks ago.

We have to pass _____ courses.

I need a _____ of graduation.

Yesterday I was _____ English class.

Our school _____ will be closed 10 p.m.

You don't have to pay _____ fee at the dormitory.

A lot of food is available in the _____.

I want to know about _____ aid program.

Fall _____ will be start September 2.

We have to take 110 _____ to get the degree.

Choose the best answer to each question

Students are asked to make sure that they do not leave their cars parked in the Liberty Hall's lot. The parking lot is scheduled to be resurfaced on Tuesday. If you need to come into the school office on Tuesday and Friday, please park at the Truth lot rather than at the Liberty lot. For the security and your safety, you may not park the white zone. The zone is for loading and unloading passengers only. Thank you for your cooperation.

1. What is going to happen on Tuesday?

   (A) There will be no classes.

   (B) Students will fix their cars.

   (C) A Parking lot will be resurfaced.

   (D) Students will go to the park with teachers.

2. Where can Students park their car on Wednesday?

   (A) At the Rheman lot.

   (B) At the Molly lot.

   (C) At the park.

   (D) On the street.

Picture Description

Describe the given picture with one sentence.

1. _____

2. _____

3.

4.

5. _____

Questions and Responses

Response the given question

1. Why are you so angry?

_____

2. How long does this program go on?

_____

3. Are there any messages for me?

_____

4. Where would you like to visit?

_____

5. Can I make a reservation?

_____

Short Conversations

Answer to each question

M: Has the part which I ordered arrived yet?

W: Not really, but they called and said that they sent it yesterday by express. I think it'll be arriving today.

M: I hope so. The customer wants to pick his car up tomorrow morning.

1. Where does this conversation take place?

_____

M: Who proofread this report?

W: Michelle did. Are there any problems?

M: Yeah. There are five mistakes on the first page alone. Maybe her mind was elsewhere while she was doing this.

2. What is the man complaining about?

_____

M: Let me help you with your bag, ma'am?

W: Thanks, but I can handle it myself.

M: Well, here's your key. Enjoy your stay.

3. What does the man offer to do for the woman?

_____

M: Do you have any ideas for a new office.

W: Why? Will you move to another place?

   I heard there is a lot of office space downtown.

   If you want, I'll find out for you.

M: Thanks a lot. But the problem is that we don't have

   enough money in the budget to move downtown.

   What about the rural area?

4. What is the man going to do?

_____

W: Oh, no! I lost my keys again!

M: Are these yours? I found them on the floor.

W: Oh, yes. Thank you so much.

5. What had the woman done?

_____

Fairy tale

Main Words (Fairy tale)

fiction	magic
lie	fairy
story	castle
island	fantasy
tradition	ghost
invention	myth
legend	fable
untruth	fork
prince	animal
flower	lesson

Fill in the blank with a suitable word

All the animals are personalized in the _____.

Life is sometimes a kind of _____.

There is a Korean _____ village at Suwon.

Most of fairy tales give a lot of life _____to people.

A lot of gods was from the Greek and Rome _____.

Many _____ animal are from the Walt Disney movies.

He is a _____ of sports.

Mobile phone is a great _____ at this time.

We often build up a sand _____.

The story is from the _____.

Once upon a time, there were an ant and a grasshopper.

One summer day, they met together at a forest.

The ant was working hard, but the grasshopper was sitting on the tree.

"Hey ant! Why are you working so hard?

Take a break, summer will be long." said the grasshopper.

"I don't think so. I should work as hard as I can." said the ant.

"Ok, keep working, I will just sit here some more."

The grasshopper ignored the ant's word.

At last, winter came. The grasshopper was very hungry.

But, he didn't have any food to eat.

So, he went to the ant's house to get some food.

The kind ant gave him some food.

The grasshopper realized he was so stupid.

1. When did the ant work so hard?

   (A) one summer day   (B) one spring day

   (C) one fall day   (D) at night

2. What did the grasshopper realize?

   (A) happiness   (B) stupidity

   (C) wonder   (D) anger

Picture Description

Describe the given picture with one sentence.

1. _____

2. _____

3. _____

4. _____

5.

Questions and Responses

Response the given question

1. Can I take my room key?

_____

2. What are you going to do this weekend?

_____

3. How long does it take to fix the machine?

_____

4. Where did you get the news?

_____

5. Can I make a reservation?

_____

Short Conversations

Answer to each question

W: Hey, Jack. Could you give me a hand to carry this box?

   I have to give this to the manager.

M: I'm really sorry. It won't be possible for the next ten minutes.

W: That's ok. There's no rush. I can

1. Who will carry the box?

_____

W: When do you think I can pick up my car?

M: It'll take two days. Can you come back Wednesday afternoon?

W: I don't think I can. I'll go out of town Tuesday and come back Thursday.

   I'll drop by Friday.

2. When will the car be ready to be picked up?

_____

W: What's the purpose of this trip?

M: I'm here for the contract. I work for Progressive

which is the biggest distributor of auto parts in Canada.

W: How long do you think will you stay?

3. What is the man doing?

_____

W: I think I'll enroll in the fitness club. I'm getting fat.

I need to work out.

M: You still look beautiful and in shape.

W: No kidding. You can't have an objective point

of view because you are my father.

4. What are they discussing?

_____

M: Thank you so much for looking after my dog while

I was away on my trip.

W: Don't mention it. I really had a good time with your dog.

I think I'll buy a dog for myself.

M: Oh, really? One of my friends runs a pet shop.

Why don't we go there right now.

5. What are they going to do?

_____

Lesson
3

Trip

Main Words (Trip)

tour	journey
guidebook	map
culture	village
budget	recommend
itinerary	schedule
field trip	brochure
observation	sightseeing
package	tour
agent	travel
agency	insurance
exchange	charge

Fill in the blank with a suitable word

I am going to make a _____ to the mountain.

We have to bring a _____ to find the village.

I have enough _____ to go Japan.

They are going to join the _____ tour.

You had better call the travel _____.

Which country do you _____?

Do you have any _____ for the museum?

We are going to do a lot of _____ on our vacation.

We have to check the _____ policy.

My travel _____ is the same as yours.

Choose the best answer to each question

Welcome to everyone who is visiting our pre-school this morning. This is vice president Kim. Let me tell you today's schedule. First, you will receive a general description of our school. During this time I'd like to explain our school system and our facilities with brochure. In this time I'll make a cyber presentation. Then I will take you to several classrooms for your observation. After that, you'll meet our president at a snack room. I want you to have a nice time. Thank you.

1. Where are they?

   (A) At a pre-school   (B) At a garden

   (C) At a hospital   (D) At a mall

2. What will they do after receiving a general description?

   (A) They will have lunch.

   (B) They will go to a classroom

   (C) They will see the plant

   (D) They will have a quick break

3. Which one will not be used by Mrs Kim to explain?

   (A) A brochure   (B) A projector

   (C) A board   (D) A computer

Picture Description

Describe the given picture with one sentence.

1. _____

2. _____

3.

4.

5. _____

Questions and Responses

Response the given question

1. Would you like a round-trip ticket?

_____

2. What do you think about the game?

_____

3. What time does the train arrive?

_____

4. Where can I get the pamphlet?

_____

5. May I ask a favor of you?

_____

Short Conversations

Answer to each question.

M: I plan to go camping with Mark this Saturday.
   Are you interested in that?

W: I'd love to. But my mother's expecting me to go shopping with her. I'll take
   a rain check.

M: That's ok.

1. What is the woman going to do on Saturday?

_____

M: I have to vacate my place at the end of the next month.

W: Why? Has the contract expired?

M: No, my landlord wants to remodel the apartment.

2. What is the man going to do?

_____

W: Could you make five copies of this paper?

M: I'd love to. But I can't. I just heard that the copy machine was broken this morning.

W: Oh, gee. And then you'd better go to the Office Max to copy rather than wait until the technician comes.

3. What can be said about the man?

_____

M: Do you carry cards? I need to write some thank-you-notes.

W: We have a large selection of cards over there.

You can choose what you like in aisle two.

M: Thank you.

4. Where are the speakers?

_____

M: Congratulations! They told me about
your promotion to be the vice president.
W: Thanks. But I have to wait until
the board of committee approves.
M: Everyone said it's a matter of time.

5. Which is true about the conversation?

_____

Lesson
4

Award

Main Words (Award)

prize	award
film	drama
play	confer
honour	national
actor	actress
producer	festival
costume	picture
win	exhibition
art	education
outstanding	cartoon

Fill in the blank with a suitable word

He was nominated for the best actor _____.

The president _____ a bachelor degree on me.

Busan film _____ takes place in October every year.

The teacher changed his _____ for the party.

The professor won an award for a _____ article.

The _____ includes Korean works.

Walt Disney _____ is known to at the Film industry.

It is a great _____ for me to win the prize.

Who is a _____ of the famous drama?

Vocational _____ is very important for getting a job.

Choose the best answer to each question

I am very happy to tell you about the winning of national president's prize. One of our teacher Min got President' prize yesterday. We all knew his dedication to our school and many students over the thirty years that he worked here. He started as a temporary teacher when our school was established and was promoted as a teacher within 2 years. He was the history of our school. The ceremony will be held this Sunday at Liberty hall and many alumni will be attended. Our principal will confer the prize to him instead of the president.

1. What is the tone of the speaker?

    (A) Happy   (B) Solemn

    (C) Annoyed   (D) Thankful

2. What was Min's position?

    (A) A board member   (B) CEO

    (C) Teacher   (D) Doctor

3. What can be inferred from this announcement?

    (A) The school will donate money

    (B) Employees will be promoted

    (C) Alumni will attend the ceremony

    (D) Employees will not go to the ceremony

Picture Description

Describe the given picture with one sentence.

1. _____

2. _____

3. _____

4. _____

5. _____

Questions and Responses

Response the given question.

1. Could you please open the window?

_____

2. Are you ready to order?

_____

3. Could you tell me where I am?

_____

4. What's the problem with your car?

_____

5. Can I give you a piece of advice?

_____

Short Conversations

Answer to each question.

W: Hi, how do you feel today?

M: I fell much better, but I still have a pain in my back.

W: Don't push yourself too hard. You need to take a rest for a while.

1. What is the relationship between the man and the woman?

_____

M: Did you see the flyer in the newspaper? Ames has already started a clearance sale on the winter stuff. Why don't we stop by to buy a heater. We need to buy another one for the winter.

W: As you know, it started last Friday and there are only two days left.

M: I know, but I think it's worth driving to.

2. What are they talking about?

_____

W: I want to refund for this shirt. I found that there is a spot and it doesn't come out.

M: I know. How about exchanging it for another one?

W: No, thanks. I'd like a refund.

3. What is the woman doing?

_____

M: Hello, is Mary there?

W: I'm sorry. There's no one here by that name.

M: I'm really sorry. I'll check the number again.

4. What is the problem?

_____

M: Please tell me about today's schedule.

W: At 9:30, you have a meeting with the prospective
contractors and a luncheon with board members at 11:30.
Finally, from 2:30 to 3:30, there is a sales meeting
for the Fall you have to chair.

M: O. K. thanks. It'll be another busy day.

5. What time will the man attend the sales meeting?

Lesson
5

Vacation

Main Words (Vacation)

reservation	block
depart	cost
fare	ticket
round trip	valuables
discount	menu
meal	breakfast
dinner	rental
policy	restaurant
rent	signature
receipt	charge

Fill in the blank with a suitable word

I need a little _____ to clear my head.

American _____ is very famous for foreigners.

Do you have make a _____ for the restaurant?

I am going to _____ a sport car.

Don't miss your _____ at the document.

Don't miss your _____ after checking out.

The hotel _____ the room fare.

We have to have three _____ a day.

All travellers are responsible for their _____.

The building is located two _____ from our hotel.

Choose the best answer to each question

I'd like to inform all the staff members of our school's new policy on summer vacation. Effective immediately, under the new policy, you are entitled to one week paid vacation. To have a vacation you don't have to submit a written request. Just sign at the office at least a month in advance. It is impossible to take more than one week vacation. If you don't have to take vacation, you can be paid small amount of money at the end of August.

1. What is the purpose of this announcement?
   (A) To give information
   (B) To ask a favor
   (C) To suggest a good idea
   (D) To enroll in the vacation program

2. When do the employees have to sign for their vacation?
   (A) A week before
   (B) Two weeks before
   (C) A month before
   (D) Two months before

Picture Description

Describe the given picture with one sentence.

1. _____

2. _____

3. _____

4. _____

5. _____

Questions and Responses

Response the given question

1. Would you like any dessert?

_____

2. Can you be back before lunch?

_____

3. Where did you go last night?

_____

4. Are you a vegetarian?

_____

5. Do you have any bags to check?

_____

Short Conversations

Answer to each question

W: Oh, gee. I am locked out again.

M: Don't worry about that. I'll be able to go in through the window.

    And I'll open it.

W: Thank so much. But you don't need to. I'll call the landlord.

1. What is the woman going to do?

_____

W: Do you have any idea what I can do about my printer. It's not working again.

M: Why don't you ask Tom. I guess he'll be able to fix it.

    He knows a lot about electronics.

W: I already did. But this is beyond his ability. I think I'll call an technician.

2. Who will repair the printer?

_____

W: Excuse me, where can I find the Geico Insurance Company building?

M: It's going to be easy. Do you see that Art Museum? It's between the fire station and the Art Museum. It's just five minutes on foot.

W: Thanks. I think I can't miss it.

3. Where is the woman looking for?

_____

M: Do you happen to know anyone who is looking for a secondhand car?

W: How about putting an ad on the local paper? You can advertise for a very resonable cost.

M: I really appreciate your information. But for now I'll try to find someone myself before advertising.

4. What does the man want to do?

_____

W: Why didn't you call me up last night, Terrence? You said you wanted to hear my opinion about the project.

M: I tried to reach you so many times but every time I called, the line was busy.

W: Oh, was it? I'm really sorry about that. I thought you deliberately didn't call me.

5. Why couldn't the man reach the woman?

_____

Lesson
6

Airport

Main Words (Airport)

destination	baggage
weight	flight
class	confirmation
board	economy
currency	customs
declaration	prohibit
limit	claim
carousel	gate
cart	transfer
passport	immigration

Fill in the blank with a suitable word

My _____ was late one hour.

I don't have any _____.

I always travel business _____.

_____ rate is very important for travellers.

You will go through _____.

You will get your baggage from the _____.

We have to _____ here.

Do you have any problem in _____.

Your boarding _____ is B205.

Where can I find a _____ for my luggage.

Choose the best answer to each question

Pay attention to the passengers for Baeseok Airlines flight 153. The flight scheduled for 2 p.m. is delayed due to the terrible snowstorm. You are requested to go to the Baeseok Airlines ticket counter. Then, you'll receive a coupon for dinner which can be used in several restaurants in the airport. Boarding time has been rescheduled for 7:30 p.m. Boarding gate will be B26. We will announce you if there are any further schedule changes. We sincerely regret any inconvenience caused by this delay. Please remind rescheduled your flight.

1. What are the passengers going to do?
   (A) To refund their ticket
   (B) Go to the gate to board
   (C) To wait in the waiting room
   (D) Go to the ticket counter

2. What will the passengers be given?
   (A) An embarkation card
   (B) A brochure for the schedule
   (C) Dinner
   (D) A boarding pass

Picture Description

Describe the given picture with one sentence.

1. _____

2. _____

3.

4.

5.

Questions and Responses

Response the given question

1. Could you ask him to proofread the article?

_____

2. How often do you play golf?

_____

3. Where can I check out?

_____

4. Will you be back in time for the party?

_____

5. Are you going to work overtime tonight?

_____

Short Conversations

Answer to each question

W: Brian, you need to have everything mailed by this Friday.

M: Yeah, I know. I'm a little worried that I'll not be able to meet the deadline. How about hiring a temporary employee for this job?

W: The company doesn't want to spend more money. I think you will have to work overtime.

1. What does the man suggest?

_____

M: When is your sabbatical?

W: From next semester, for one year.

M: I have to wait several years for mine. I really need to have some time off.

2. What is a sabbatical?

_____

W: What time does Macy's open?

M: It usually opens at 10 a.m. But the ad said it would open an hour earlier during the clearance sale.

W: It's already 9:30. Let's hurry.

3. What time does Macy's open?

_____

W: It's a perfect meal in a very beautiful garden with a pond. Did you prepare it yourself?

M: Almost. My wife gave me a hand.

W: I can barely boil water.

4. What is true about the woman?

_____

M: Here's your ticket and itinerary.

W: Thanks, Mr. Henry. We couldn't go home on time without your help.

M: I enjoy helping all my clients.

5. What is the man's occupation?

_____

Leisure

Main Words (Leisure)

adult	admission
height	restriction
discount	available
cash	locker
possession	locker
soda	change
purchase	amusement
rate	event
membership	benefit
thrill	entertainment

Fill in the blank with a suitable word

Food _____ is normal at a amusement park.

We will give _____ for you.

A lot of food are _____ in the park.

People can leave their possession in the _____.

You need to keep the receipt as proof of _____.

Do you have any sport _____.

What kind of _____ can you suggest?

The movie was a big _____.

Please, keep the _____.

What kind of _____ are there at night?

Choose the best answer to each question

Thank you for calling us. You have reached Baeseok amusement park. We always do our best for your satisfaction. If you would like to purchase tickets, press one. If you would like to know about special events, press two. If you would like to know about rates, press three. If you would like directions and information about parking, press four. If you would like to know our opening hours, press five. If you would like to speak to the operator, press zero. Thank you for calling us again.

1. If you would like to know the price, which button should you press?

   (A) One   (B) Two

   (C) Three   (D) Four

2. If you do not know the way to the zoo, Which button should you press?

   (A) Two   (B) Three

   (C) Four   (D) Five

3. If you want to talk with the operator, what should you do?

   (A) Wait   (B) Press two

   (C) Press zero   (D) Call again

Picture Description

Describe the given picture with one sentence.

1. _____

2. _____

3. _____

4. _____

5. _____

Questions and Responses

Response the given question

1. Why don't we take a break?

_____

2. Where can I leave my bag?

_____

3. May I speak with John?

_____

4. Are you going to open your account?

_____

5. Could you tell me your office hours?

_____

Short Conversations

Answer to each question

M: When is your appointment, Ms. Sarkelra?

W: Actually, it's 11 a.m. tomorrow. But I can't stand the pain in my mouth. Can I see Dr. Johnson sometime this morning?

M: I'll check to see if she is available.

1. Who does the man want to see?

_____

W: The company decided to cut down the benefits yesterday.

M: I also heard that they are planning to lay off some workers.

W: I hope we get over the recession soon.

2. What are they talking about?

_____

M: Alyssa, what will you bring to the potluck at Armanda's place this Saturday?

W: Well, I think I will make an apple pie. What about you?

M: I'm not sure yet.

3. What are they talking about?

_____

M: Something's wrong with this. I already set it for letter size and pressed the start button.

W: You have to put in more paper, that's why.

M: I didn't notice that. thanks.

4. What is the man going to use?

_____

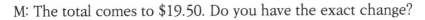

M: The total comes to $19.50. Do you have the exact change?

W: Sorry, I have only a 20-dollar bill. And then,

can I have some quarters in change?

M: I have only 10-cent coins. Are they ok?

5. What does the customer want for change?

_____

Telephone

Main Words (Telephone)

urgent	message
hang on	hold on
contact	connect
confirm	apology
polite	etiquette
official	private
public	mobil phone
button	transmission
call	phone
operator	appointment

Fill in the blank with a suitable word

Are there a _____ for me today?

I will _____ you to my boss.

We have to be _____ to ask something.

Many _____ suffer from a mental illness.

Phone _____ is very important at a public place.

Please, press _____ 1 to buy it.

Call 119 when it is _____.

I want to _____ my booking day.

If you have a question, please _____ me at anytime.

We have to be polite talking on the _____.

Choose the best answer to each question

Hi, Mr. Kim. This is Ami, the receptionist, at Dr. Jun's Dental Clinic. I'm calling about your appointment. You were supposed to see the doctor on Tuesday, May 15th at 11 a.m.. The doctor will be out of the office that week because of personal affairs. And so your appointment has been changed to May 22th at 11 a.m.. This is just a reminder that your appointment is one week later than planned. If you have any problem that day, please, call this number. We can adjust your appointment. I am sorry to change your time. Have a nice day!

1. Who left this message?
   (A) A doctor
   (B) A nurse
   (C) A receptionist
   (D) Keats

2. What is the purpose of this message?
   (A) To cancel his appointment with doctor
   (B) To inform that the doctor will be on vacation
   (C) To persuade Mrs. Ami to join the party
   (D) To tell Mrs. Ami about the changed schedule

Picture Description

Describe the given picture with one sentence.

1. _____

2. _____

3. _____

4. _____

5.

Questions and Responses

Response the given question

1. Can you finish it by on Friday?

_____

2. Will you be able to do it?

_____

3. Are you ready to go?

_____

4. Could you pass me the sugar?

_____

5. Could you tell her to call me?

_____

Short Conversations

Answer to each question

M: It rains a lot. I think we have to call off the picnic to the lake tomorrow.

W: I saw the weather report just before. The weather man said it's going to be cloudy and windy in the morning. And it'll be a hot day like a typical summer day.

M: Then, we don't need to change our schedule.

1. What will be the weather like tomorrow afternoon?

_____

W: Did you hear the news about the Yankees?

M: Yes, they said they decided to recruit a Korean pitcher named Kim. The reporter was convinced it would be another successful year with Kim.

W: I hope so.

2. What are the Yankees going to do?

_____

M: Tomorrow is our Town's festival. This year, we'll have a firework and food contest.

W: Fireworks, wow! Sounds great! What time will the firework begin, you know?

M: I heard it begins at 8 o'clock and goes to 11 p.m.

3. What are they talking about?

_____

M: May I speak to Mr. Kawasaki?

W: Hang on a second. I'll see if he's available. Oh, his line is busy. May I take a message?

M: Could you just tell him I'm the one who applied for the temporary job.

4. What is Mr. Kawasaki doing?

_____

M: What's your speech topic on the history class next Monday.

W: I have chosen Napoleon. So, now I'm studying French history. There are tons of books I have to read.

M: It's going to be tough, but it gives you so much knowledge. Good for you.

5. What is the man going to do until next Monday?

_____

Business

Main Words (Business)

industry	product
franchise	corporate
appliance	ownership
annual	performance
refund	shipping
inspection	function
organization	expert
deal	operate
company	consumer
agreement	estimate

Fill in the blank with a suitable word

The famous ice cream _____ made a big profit.

Government announces the _____ health report.

You have to pay the _____ charge.

They _____ many book stores in Korea.

Two companies were satisfied with the _____.

Companies have to be responsive to _____ demand.

People have to take a medical _____ every other year.

Many people use a _____ card.

Could you send me the _____ of the car.

There is no _____ the goods.

Choose the best answer to each question

Subway is best-known and most successful businesses in the food, and Starbucks is the same as it in the beverage industry. They were founded in American.

Both of them have successfully extended to international markets such as Korea, Canada and Japan.

One sells coffee and the other sells sandwiches as its core product. While Starbucks has kept its now more than 36,000 chain stores corporate-owned in the world, Subway has run by franchised stores.

These two business models have their own advantages and challenges. While Starbucks now runs more than 36,000 outlets world, Subway opened 44,000 stores. There are about 1,200 Starbucks stores and 450 Subway stores in Korea.

1. What's the subway's core goods?

   (A) food   (B) sandwiches

   (C) ice cream   (D) coffee

2. How many shops does Starbucks run in the world ?

   (A) 36,000   (B) 44,000

   (C) 1,200   (D) None

Picture Description

Describe the given picture with one sentence.

1.
_____

2.
_____

3. _____

4. _____

5.

Questions and Responses

Response the given question

1. Where's my ring?

_____

2. Can you play the piano?

_____

3. What are you going to do?

_____

4. Could you change fifty dollars?

_____

5. Can you type this letter?

_____

Short Conversations

Answer to each question

M: I'd like to rent a car for this weekend.

W: What kind of car do you have in mind?

M: I don't need a full-sized car. we are just two. So a compact car with a ski rack will be ok.

1. Where is the man going to go for the weekend?

_____

M: We really enjoyed the meal. Do you accept credit cards?

W: Yes, we absolutely do, but temporarily it's not possible to use any credit cards because something's wrong with the machine. If you pay in cash, we'll give you 5 percent off instead.

M: That's much better.

2. What is the problem?

_____

W: What's the matter with you, Dave? You look upset.

M: I'm feeling under the weather. I think I'd better quit for the day.

W: Don't worry. I'll tell the director for you and he'll understand.

3. What is the true?

_____

M: I'm calling about the advertisement. Is the two beds still available?

W: Yes, it is. It's really spacious and clean. The best thing is that it has a view of
the river.

M: Great. And how about the utilities and security deposit?

4. What does the man want to do?

_____

M: My flight was overbooked again, and the take-off was delayed an hour. I can't stand this.

W: That's weird. I always use that airline but this has never happened.

M: If it happens again, I'll never fly with them.

5. What makes the man upset?

_____

Part

II

Grammar

영어 문장구조
(sentence Structure)

영어 문장구조(sentence Structure)

의미: 다른 나라 언어와 마찬가지로, 영어 문장이 되기 위해서는 일정한 구조적인 규칙을 가지고 있으며, 이 규칙에 따라 문장을 사용 할 때 비로써 의미를 확정한다.

(1) 문장의 구성요소 및 성분

① 문장의 구성 요소: 단어, 구, 절

단어: 말의 최소 단위로서 영어에서는 그 특성(품사)에 따라 8가지로 구분

I <u>love</u> <u>peace</u>.

구(Phrase): 두개 이상의 단어가 한 덩어리가 되어 의미를 갖는 것

My mother <u>take care of</u> many children.

절(Clause): 두개 이상의 단어가 한 덩어리가 되어 의미를 가지면서,
주어와 술어관계가 되어 하나의 문장(말)이 되는 것

I think <u>the boy is honest</u>.

* 단어의 특성 (품사): 모든 단어는 8가지 특성으로 구분되며, 이것을 "품사"라고 한다.

명사: 사람, 사물 등 유·무형을 지칭

예) book, family, love, water, Seoul

대명사: 명사를 대신해서 받는 것

예) I, you, he, she, they, we, it

동사: 동작이나 상태를 나타내 는 것

예) go, come, run, study, see, eat

형용사: 명사의 성질이나 상태를 나타냄

예) beautiful, good, kind, happy, honest

부사: 여러 다른 품사의 상태를 나타내고, 장소, 방법, 시간, 이유 등을 표현

예) very, pretty, easily, fast, happily

접속사: 단어와 단어, 구와 구, 절과 절 등을 연결

예) and, or, but, that, because,

전치사: 명사를 목적어로 해서 기본 문장을 확장

예) in, at, on, from, for

감탄사: 놀람이나 감탄을 나타낸다.

예) wow, oh

② 문장 성분: 문장에서 어떤 쓰임을 하느냐에 따라 주어, 술어(동사), 목적어,
  보어 등으로 구분하는데 이를 문장 성분이라 한다.

주어: 문장의 주체로서 "은/는/이/가"로 해석

동사(술어): 문장을 서술해 주는 것으로서 "--다"로 해석

보어: 주어나 목적어를 설명하는 것

목적어: 주어 행위의 대상으로서 "--에게" 또는 "을/를"로 해석

I painted the door green.

(I: 주어, painted: 동사, the door:목적어, green:보어)

(2) 문장의 기본 구조(문장의 5가지 형태)

모든 영어 문장은 5가지 구조를 가지고 있는데, 이것을 문장의 5형식 이라고 하며 1형
식문장, 2형식문장, 3형식문장, 4형식문장, 5형식문장이라고 각각 말해진다.

① 1형식: 주어 + 동사 (Subject + Verb)

The sun rises.

Birds sing.

My father works.

② 2형식: 주어 + 동사 + 보어 (S + V + Complement)

I am happy.

He became a doctor.

She looks happy.

She appears sensible.

* 대표적인 2형식 동사

be, become, go, grow, look, appear, seem, remain

③ 3형식: 주어 + 동사 + 목적어 (S + V + Object)

I like apples.

I met him.

They helped the man.

I finished the project.

④ 4형식: 주어 + 동사 + 간접목적어 + 직접목적어

(S + V + O + Indirect Object + Direct Object)

I gave her the book.

      → I gave the book to her.(3형식)

He sent the patient flowers.

      → He sent flowers to the patient.(3형식)

Linda teaches us English.

      → Linda teaches English to us.(3형식)

* 4형식을 3 형식으로 고칠 때 to를 사용하지 않는 동사

buy, build, make, get, order, cook, receive : for + I.O.

    I'll make some coffee for you.

ask, require, beg, demand, inquire : of + I.O.

    He asked a question of me.

play, impose, confer : on + I.O.

    He played a trick on me.

    They imposed a tax of 100 dollars on me.

⑤ 5형식: 주어 + 동사 + 목적어 + 보어 (S + V + O + C)

We elected him president.

I found this book easy.

I painted the desk blue.

They believed the boy honest.

(3) 동사의 종류

동사를 분류하는 데는 다양한 방법이 있는데, 문장을 만들 때는 동사(술어)가 그 다음에 오는 문장성분을 선택하게 된다. 따라서 문장을 만들 때에는 동사의 선택이 중요하며, 동사의 선택에 따라 문장이 구분되어 만들어 진다.

자동사: 목적어를 선택하지 않는 동사

The earth <u>moves</u>. (1형식)

She <u>became</u> a singer. (2형식)

타동사: 목적어를 선택하는 동사

I don't <u>know</u> the doctor. (3형식)

The boy <u>sent</u> the girl a present. (4형식)

We <u>called</u> him a fool. (5형식)

A. 밑 줄 친 단어의 품사를 구분하세요.

1. I forgot to book a <u>ticket</u> for the movie.
2. I am going to meet him <u>at</u> the coffee shop.
3. Mary <u>and</u> Tom look very happy.
4. He showed her an <u>expensive</u> computer.
5. English is not <u>so</u> easy for me.
6. The man invited <u>my</u> sister yesterday.

B. 아래 문장에서 밑줄 친 동사를 자동사와 타동사로 구분하세요.

1. He <u>smiles</u> at me.
2. We <u>made</u> a reservation.
3. They <u>went</u> to the park in the morning.
4. I <u>found</u> the book difficult.
5. They don't <u>want</u> to take a bus.

C. 아래 문장이 몇 형식 문장인지 구분하세요.

1. The beautiful bird is singing on the tree.
2. I thought it a dog.
3. The man killed himself on Monday.
4. Seoul is the capital of Korea.
5. Could you lend me your pen?

영어 문장의 종류
(Types of sentence)

영어 문장의 종류(Types of sentence)

의미: 의사표현을 하는 데 있어, 말을 하는 사람이 상대방에게 어떤 사실이나, 상태를 자신의 의도에 따라 구분해서 문장을 선택하며, 4가지로 구분된다.

평서문: 어떤 사실이나 상태를 평범하게 나타내는 문장
의문문: 어떤 사실이나 상태에 대해 의견 또는 대답을 요구하는 문장
명령문: 말하는 이가 자신 또는 듣는 사람에게 무엇을 시키거나 행동을 요구하는 문장
감탄문: 자신의 감정이나 느낌을 감탄하여 표현하는 문장

* 긍정문과 부정문: 위 문장들을 때로는 긍정문으로 때로는 부정문으로 표현하게 되며, 이에 대한 구분

(1) 평서문: 주어+동사의 어순으로 쓴다.

The lion runs very fast.

I am very happy.

Billy loved Jane at that time.

She bought him a bicycle.

They made her sad.

He can speak English very well.

* 평서문의 부정문 만들기

① be 동사가 있는 평서문: be동사 뒤에 not을 붙인다.

He is a doctor.

　　→ He is not a doctor.

The cat is dangerous.

　　→ The cat is not dangerous.

② 조동사가 있는 평서문: 조동사 뒤에 not을 붙인다.

He can speak English.

　　　→ He can't speak English.

We will meet the mayor at the city hall.

　　　→ We will not meet the mayor at the city hall.

③ 일반 동사가 있는 평서문: "do" 동사를 일반동사 앞에 넣고 do동사 다음에 not를 붙인다.

I want to study with him.

　　　→ I don't want to study with him.

Linda loves John.

　　　→ Linder does not love John.

They made her sad.

　　　→ They did not make her sad.

(2) 의문문: 의문사 있는 의문문과 의문사 없는 의문문으로 구분되며, 동사 + 주어의 어순을 갖는다.

① 의문사 없는 의문문: 주어와 동사의 어순이 동사 + 주어의 순서가 된다.

　ⓐ be 동사가 있는 평서문: be동사가 문장 앞으로 간다.

She is a famous singer.

　　　→ Is she a famous singer?

They are angry.

　　　→ Are they angry?

　ⓑ 조동사가 있는 평서문: 조동사가 문장 앞으로 간다.

They can play the piano.

　　　→ Can they play the piano.

He will write a novel.

　　　→ Will he write a novel.

ⓒ 일반 동사가 있는 평서문: "do" 동사를 문장 앞에 넣고, 원래 있던 동사는
"원형"을 사용한다.

I met the woman.

　　→ Did I meet her?

She teaches him English.

　　→ Does she teach him English?

They elected the man mayor.

　　→ Did they elect the man mayor?

② 의문사 있는 의문문: When, Where, Who, What, How, Why 등의 의문사가 있는
의문문으로서, 의문사는 항상 문두에 위치하며,
동사 + 주어의 어순을 유지한다.

When do you want to go there?

Where is the police station?

Who is the man over there?

What shall I do next time?

How can I help you?

Why are they so excited?

(3) 명령문: 명령뿐만 아니라 청유, 정중한 부탁(간접명령)도 포함되며,
일반적으로 상대방에게 지시하는 것이기 때문에
주어 "You"가 생략되어 동사원형으로 시작된다.

Do it yourself.

Open the door, please.

Let me introduce myself.

Let me say.

* 명령문 다음에 오는 "and" 는 '그러면'으로 "or"는 '그러지 않으면"으로 해석

Study hard, and you will pass the test.

Work hard, or you will be fired.

**(4) 감탄문: 평서문을 사용해서 감탄을 나타내기도 하고,
        "how"나 "what"을 사용해서 감탄을 표현한다.**

You are so beautiful!

What a nice day it is!

    (What a/an 명사 주어 동사)

How pretty it is!

    (How 형용사 주어 동사)

A. 아래 문장의 종류를 구분하세요.

평서문, 의문문, 명령문, 감탄문

1. What a kind man he is!
2. Did you meet him yesterday?
3. Let him go.
4. Is she a teacher?
5. The program is very useful.

B. 아래문장들을 부정문으로 만드세요.

1. My uncle was very diligent.
2. My sister watched the T.V show yesterday.
3. They paint the roof white.
4. William sent Linda the jewelry box.
5. I can do it.

C. 아래 문장들을 의문문으로 만드세요.

1. He is interested in politics.
2. Susan is from America.
3. She likes to talk on the phone.
4. Birds sing in the forest.
5. She will do her best tomorrow.

명사
(Noun)

명사(Noun)

의미: 사람, 사물, 유·무형을 말하는 단어

역할: 문장에서 주어, 목적어, 보어 역할

명사의 종류

셀 수 있는 명사: 문장에서 단수, 복수 구분을 해야 한다. 보통명사, 집합명사

셀 수 없는 명사: 단수 취급을 하며, 복수형을 만들 수 없다. 물질명사, 추상명사, 고유

명사

(1) 보통명사: 같은 종류의 사람, 사물, 동물에 공통적으로 붙일 수 있는 명사

예) book, pen, desk, house, room, door, window, board, projector

I read a book.

He likes apples.

(2) 집합명사: 사람, 또는 사물의 집합체를 나타내는 명사

① 집합체의 단일성을 강조하면, 단수취급

② 집합체의 개별성을 강조하면 복수취급

예) family, public, audience, team, committee, faculty

His family is very large

His family get up all early in the morning.

The committee meets once a week.

The committee express their opinions at the meeting.

(3) 물질명사: 일정한 모양을 갖추지 않은 물질을 나타내는 명사

예) water, tea, coffee, paper, oil, milk, sugar, salt, money, sand

Milk is made into butter and cheese.

This box was made of paper.

* 물질명사의 수량 표시

a glass of water,   two glasses of water

a sheet of paper,   three sheets of paper

a bottle of beer,   two bottles of beer

a cup of coffee,   two cups of coffee

a pound of sugar,   two pounds of sugar

(4) 추상명사: 눈으로 볼 수도 없고 손으로 만질 수도 없는 추상적인 무형의 명사
원칙적으로 관사를 사용할 수 없으며, 복수형도 되지 않는다.

예) art, beauty, wisdom, truth, love, honesty, peace, news, youth, time, success, failure

Life is short and art is long

The man was wild in his youth.

* 추상명사의 수량 표시

a piece of information

a piece of news

a piece of advice

(5) 고유명사 : 특정한 사람, 사물, 장소, 회사에 쓰이는 고유한 이름 나타내는 명사

Hanlasan is the highest mountain in Korea.

Shakespeare is an excellent writer.

Samsung is a big company.

명사의 수

셀 수 있는 명사 (보통명사, 집합명사)는 문장에서 사용 될 때, 단수인지 복수인지를 확인하여 사용해야한다. 단 셀 수 없는 명사는 원칙적으로 단수로만 사용된다.

명사의 복수형 만들기

(1) 규칙변화

① 대부분의 단어 끝에 -s 를 붙인다.

예) books, doctors, students, pens, apples, tigers, lions, sons, flowers

② 어미가 -s, -ss, -x, -sh, -ch로 끝나면 -es를 붙인다.

예) buses, glasses, boxes, dishes, benches, peaches, brushes

③ 자음 + y 로 끝나는 단어는 y 를 i 로 고친 뒤 -es 를 붙인다.

예) ladies, cities, babies, soliloquies, duties, flies

④ 「자음 + o」는 -es를 붙인다.

예) potatoes, heroes, negroes, echoes

* 주의 : 「자음 + o」 라도 -s 만 붙이는 경우가 있다.

예) pianos, solos, autos, photos, memos, sopranos

⑤ 어미가 -f(e) 로 끝나면 -f를 -ves로 고친다.

예) lives, thieves, knives, leaves, wives, wolves, shelves

* 주의 : roofs, chiefs, safes, cliffs, proofs

(2) 불규칙변화

① 모음을 변화시켜 복수로 만드는 경우

예) 모음변화 : men, feet, women, geese, teeth, mice

② -en, -ren 을 붙여 복수로 만드는 경우

예) children, oxen

③ 단수와 복수의 형태가 같은 단어

예) sheep, deer, salmon, trout, fish,

A. 아래 문장에서 명사에 밑줄을 치고, 그 종류(보통, 집합, 물질, 추상, 고유)를 쓰세요.

1. The boy wants to be a good <u>doctor</u>.
2. He ordered a cup of <u>coffee</u>.
3. The <u>audience</u> have to pay extra <u>money</u> for the concert.
4. There are many people in <u>Seoul</u>.
5. <u>Honesty</u> is very important.

B. 아래 문장에서 밑줄 친 명사가 셀 수 있는 명사인지(가산), 아닌지(불가산)를 표시하세요.

1. There are many <u>churches</u> in the city.
2. He is a smart <u>student.</u>
3. Jane loves <u>Tom</u>.
4. She went to the <u>Busan</u>.
5. We paid much <u>money</u>.
6. <u>Glass</u> is easy to break.
7. We had much <u>snow</u> last winter.
8. The traveller wanted some <u>water</u>.
9. The <u>team</u> won the game.
10. <u>Knowledge</u> is very important.

C. 아래 문장에서 밑줄 친 부분을 바르게 고치세요. 필요하면 a/an을 첨가하세요.

1. There are many <u>potato</u> in the shop.
2. Could you lend me <u>car</u>?
3. I don't understand a <u>English</u>.
4. He come from <u>a Japan</u>.
5. <u>A milk</u> is good for health.
6. The roof is covered with <u>a snow</u>.
7. There are three <u>knife</u> on the table.
8. They took care of three <u>baby</u>.

대명사
(Pronoun)

대명사(Pronoun)

의미: 명사를 대신해서 받는 단어

역할: 문장에서 주어, 목적어, 보어역할을 한다.

대명사의 종류: 인칭대명사, 지시대명사, 부정대명사

인칭 대명사

인칭		주격	소유격	목적격	소유대명사	재귀대명사
1인칭	단수	I	my	me	mine	myself
	복수	we	our	us	ours	ourselves
2인칭	단수	you	your	you	yours	yourself
	복수	you	your	you	yours	yourselves
3인칭	단수	he	his	him	his	himself
		she	her	her	hers	herself
		it	its	it		itself
	복수	they	their	them	theirs	themselves

(1) we, you, they가 일반인을 나타내는 경우가 있다.
이 때 we, you, they는 해석하지 않는 것이 자연스럽다.

We should keep our promise.

They say that he is honest.

You should not speak ill of others.

(2) 소유대명사

소유격 + 명사 = 소유대명사

Your cell phone is new, but mine is old.

(3) 재귀대명사

① **강조 용법** : 강조나 대조를 나타내기 위해 명사나 대명사 뒤에 쓰이며, 생략하여도 문법상으로 지장이 없고, 강조하는 말 뒤나 문미에 위치한다.

I myself carried the suitcase.

He did it himself.

② **재귀적 용법** : 문장의 목적어가 주어와 동일인[사물]인 경우에 쓰인다.

He killed himself.

History repeats itself.

③ **관용적 용법**

He did it for himself. (혼자 힘으로)

He went there by himself. (혼자서)

The door opened of itself. (저절로)

(4) It의 용법

① 앞에 나온 어구(명사, 구, 절)를 받는다.

I tried to open the box. but it was impossible.

② 비인칭 대명사 it : 특별히 가리키는 것이 없이, 문장을 만들기 위해서 주어 자리에 쓰는 것을 말한다. 이 때 it 는 시간, 계절, 날씨, 거리, 명암을 나타낸다.

· What time is it now? (시간)

· It is spring now. (계절)

· It is fine today. (날씨)

· How long does it take from here to the station? (거리)

· It is dark in the room. (명암)

지시 대명사

(1) this/these, that/those

① 가까운 것/ 먼 것

This is a pen.

That is a book.

② 전자/ 후자 (that / this)

He keeps one dog and one cat; this is more faithful than that.

③ 명사의 반복을 피하기 위한 that / those.

The tail of a fox is longer than that of a cat.

부정 대명사

(1) one 의 용법

① 일반적인 사람을 나타낸다. 이 때 one은 해석되지 않는다.

One should keep one's promise.

One should obey one's parents.

② 앞에 나온 명사의 반복을 피하기위해서 쓴다.

　a + 단수보통명사 : one (같은 종류의 다른 물건)

　the/this/that + 단수보통명사 : it (똑같은 바로 그 물건)

If you need a book. I will lend you one.

I bought that book, but I lost it.

(2) some과 any의 용법
　some은 긍정문에서, any는 의문문, 부정문, 조건문에 쓰인다.

Some of the employees work really hard.

He asked for some money, but I didn't give him any.

If you need any money, I'll lend some to you.

(3) all, both, every, each

① all은 가산명사와 쓰일 때는 복수취급, 불가산 명사와 쓰일 때는 단수 취급한다.

All of them were happy.

All the money was spent.

All were happy.

② 부분부정 : every, all, both 가 부정어와 같이 쓰이면 부분부정이 된다.

He didn't eat all of the tangerines.

I did not invite all of them.

Every bird can not sing.

They don't know everything.

Both of them did not come.

I do not know both of them.

A. 괄호 안에 알맞은 인칭대명사를 써 넣으세요.

1. This question is very difficult for (　　　　　).
2. This pen is (　　　　　).
3. She sent (　　　　　) a letter.
4. (　　　　　) work for Samsung.
5. The man asked me (　　　　　) address.

B. 괄호 안에 알맞은 대명사를 써 넣으세요.

1. The girl showed me a red sweater, but I didn't like (　　　　　).
2. This dog is stronger than (　　　　　).
3. They were proud of (　　　　　) for winning the game.
4, He said the bag was (　　　　　).
5. My mother bought me blue neckties, and I really like (　　　　　).
6. If you need a pen, I will give (　　　　　) to you.

C. 아래 문장에서 밑줄 친 "it"의 쓰임을 구분하세요.

1. <u>It</u> is snowing outside.
2. How far is <u>it</u> from here to the mall.
3. Tom bought a car and he drove <u>it</u> to the school.
4. <u>It</u> is April 21.
5. I tried to open the box. but <u>it</u> was impossible.
6. <u>It</u> is already five.

동사(Verb)
조동사(Modal Auxiliary)

동사(Verb)

의미: 동사는 문장을 완성 해 주며, "--다"로 해석한다.

역할: 주어의 행위, 동작, 상태를 나타내며, 문장을 지배하고, 시제를 나타낸다.

(1) 동사의 종류: be 동사, 조동사, 일반 동사

① be동사: am, are, is로서 기본적인 뜻은 "--이다" 와 " 있다"로 해석되지만, 문장에서
　　　　다양한 역할을 하므로, 특별 동사로 구분된다.

He is a student.

To be or not to be, that is a question.

There is a book on the desk.

② 조동사: 문장에서 홀로 쓰이지 못하고, 다른 동사와 함께 쓰여 내용을 보충해주는 역할
　　　　을 한다. 대표적으로 can/could, will/would, shall/should, may/might,
　　　　must, need 등이 있다.

I can speak English well.

I will do my best.

We should do study hard.

③ 일반 동사: 위 두 경우를 제외하고, "--다"로 문장에서 해석되는 동사로서, 대부분의
　　　　동사가 여기에 포함된다.

The man runs very fast.

Anton loves Jane very much.

They gave him a lot of money.

(2) 동사의 형태

① 현재형: 주어가 3인칭 단수일 때만 원칙적으로 "s" 나 "es"를 단어 끝에 붙인다.

I work for the company.

You work for the company.

They wore for the company.

He works for the company.

* 동사가 -ch, -sh, -x, -z, -s, -o로 끝나면 "-es"를 붙인다.

watch → watches / wash →washes / pass → passes,

동사가 자음 + y로 끝나면, "y"를 "i"로 고치고 "-es"를 붙인다.

carry → carries / study → studies / marry → marries

② 과거형 및 과거분사

ⓐ 규칙변화 : 원형에 '-ed'를 붙인다.

wanted, worked, closed, noticed, visited

They worked at the plant yesterday.

Many people wanted to take a trip.

My parents visited me last Sunday.

* 1 음절 어에서 모음이 하나일 경우 마지막 자음 하나를 겹쳐 쓴다.

nod - nodded -nodded / stop - stopped - stopped

beg - begged - begged / rob - robbed- robbed

* 2 음절에서는 둘째 음절에 accent가 있을 때만 자음을 겹친다.

omit - omitted - omitted / admit - admitted - admitted

prefer - preferred - preferred / occur - occurred - occurred

* 「자음 + y」인 경우는 'y'를 'i'로 고쳐서 '-ed'를 붙인다.

cry - cried - cried / try - tried - tried

study - studied - studied / carry - carried - carried

ⓑ 불규칙변화: 영어에는 약 350여개 정도의 동사가 불규칙으로 변하고 있으며, 4가지 형태로 나타난다.

ABC형 see - saw - seen / break - broke - broken

ABB형 say - said - said / bring - brought - brought

ABA형 come - came - come / run - ran - run

AAA형 put - put - put / hit - hit - hit

(3) 동사의 시제 : 12시제

단순	과거 worked	현재 work	미래 will work
완료 have + 과거분사	had worked	have worked	will have worked
진행 be + ___ing	was working	am working	will working
완료진행 have been__ing	had been working	have been working	will have been working

① 현재시제

ⓐ 현재의 동작

Here comes the teacher.

I go to school.

ⓑ 현재의 상태

It is very warm today.

He lives in Korea.

ⓒ 현재의 습관적 동작, 습관, 직업, 성질, 능력

He is often late for school.(습관적 동작)

I get up at six every morning.(습관)

He teaches English.(직업)

She laughs too much.(성질)

She types seventy words a minute.(능력)

ⓓ 불변의 진리, 사실, 속담

Man is mortal.(사람은 죽게 마련이다)

The sun rises in the east.

ⓔ 미래의 대용: 왕래발착, 시작 등을 나타내는 동사(go, come, leave, start, begin, start, arrive, return)는 미래를 나타내는 부사(구)와 함께 현재시제로 미래시제를 대신한다.

I start for Busan tomorrow.(= will start)

He comes back next week.(= will come)

The school begins next week.(= will begin)

② **과거시제**

ⓐ 과거의 동작, 상태

I was born in 1976.

He met his girl friend.

ⓑ 과거의 습관

He would often go fishing with her.

I met him very often at the bus stop.

ⓒ 역사적 사실

My teacher asked me when Columbus discovered America.

③ 미래시제: 자연현상, 가능(능력), 기대, 감정, 인간의 의지가 포함되지 않은 미래 등

    It will rain tomorrow.

    You will be sad.

    There will be no school tomorrow.

④ 현재진행

  ⓐ 지금 진행되고 있는 동작

    I am reading a novel.

    It is raining now.

    She's in her room studying.

  ⓑ 미래표시 부사(구)가 왕래발착 동사의 현재 진행형과 함께 쓰이면
    가까운 미래를 나타낸다.

    He is leaving for America soon.

    Where are you spending your next summer vacation?

* be going to + 동사원형의 용법

  ⓐ 가까운 미래 : 막 ~하려 하다. (= be about to)

    I am going to write a letter.

    It's going to rain.

  ⓑ 예정/의도 : ~할 작정/예정이다(사전 계획을 통해 미래에 하고자 하는 경우)

    I am going to stay here for a week.

    I am going to be a doctor.

  ⓒ 미래 : ~할 것이다.(= will)

    It's going to storm tomorrow.

    You are going to see him very often.

⑤ 과거진행 : 과거의 어느 시점에서 진행 중인 동작을 나타낸다.

He was reading a novel when I entered the room.

⑥ 미래진행 : 미래의 어느 시점에서 진행 중인 동작을 나타낸다.

Don't phone me between 7 and 8. We'll be having dinner then.

⑦ 현재완료 : 현재를 기준 시점으로 하여 과거의 어느 시점에서 현재까지의 완료, 결과,
　　　　경험, 계속을 나타낸다.

ⓐ 완료 : 현재에 있어 동작의 완료를 나타낸다. today, this year, recently, just,
　　　now, already, by this time, yet, so far 등과 같이 쓰인다.

I have not finished yet.

He has just come back home.

ⓑ 결과: 과거 동작에 대한 현재의 결과를 나타낸다.

He has lost his watch.(= He lost his watch and doesn't have it now)

She has bought a new car.(= She bought a new car and has it now)

She has gone to the station.(= She went to the station and is there now)

ⓒ 경험: 과거에서 현재까지의 동작, 상태의 경험을 나타낸다. ever, never, before,
　　　once, twice, several times, often, seldom 등과 같이 쓰인다.

I have never been to Europe.

Have you ever seen a tiger ?

I have met him before.

ⓓ 계속: 과거에서 현재까지의 상태의 계속을 나타낸다.

She has been ill since last week.

Five years have passed since he died.

I have known him since he was a child.

⑧ 과거완료: 과거의 어느 때를 기준점으로 하여 그 이전에 일어난 일의 동작,

　　　　혹은 상태의 완료, 결과, 경험, 계속을 나타낸다.

　ⓐ 완료

　　　He had gone to bed when I came to home.

　　　They had arrived at the house before night fell.

　ⓑ 결과

　　　Spring had come by the time she was well again.

　ⓒ 계속

　　　He had lived there for ten years when his mother died.

　ⓓ 경험

　　　I did not know him, for I had never seen him before.

⑨ 미래완료: 미래의 한 시점을 기준으로 그 때까지 일어난 동작, 혹은 상태의 완료, 결과,

　　　　계속, 경험을 나타낸다.

　　　I shall have finished the work by the time you come.(완료)

　　　When you awake, these fancies will have gone.(결과)

　　　I shall have read this book three times if I read it once again.(경험)

　　　I will have been hospital for two weeks by next Sunday.(상태계속)

⑩ 현재완료 진행: 과거의 어느 시점에서 시작되어 현재 시점에서도 계속되는 동작

　　　He has been studying for ten years.

　　　I have been reading in my study.

⑪ 과거완료 진행: 과거 이전의 어느 시점에 시작되어 일정 과거 시점에서도 계속되는 동작

　　　I had been waiting for an hour when he returned.

⑫ 미래완료진행: 미래의 한 시점에 진행되고 있을 동작

　　　I shall have been reading this novel by noon.

A. 밑줄 친 동사의 종류를 구분하세요. (be동사, 조동사, 일반 동사)

1. He <u>lives</u> in Seoul.

2. I <u>believe</u> you made a mistake.

3. The man <u>became</u> a famous artist.

4. The foreigner <u>can</u> speak Korean.

5. She has <u>finished</u> her project.

6. Edward <u>was</u> a computer programmer.

B. 밑줄 친 동사의 과거형을 쓰세요.

1. I <u>have</u> a lot of books.

2. She <u>writes</u> Harry Potter.

3. They <u>think</u> he is a doctor.

4. Many people <u>want</u> to see the game.

5. The player <u>hits</u> the ball.

6. I <u>read</u> a history novel.

C. 밑줄 친 동사의 시제를 구분하세요.

1. <u>Have</u> you ever <u>been</u> to America?

2. John <u>is staying</u> in Seoul.

3. She could not sleep well, because she <u>has had</u> much tea.

4. My brother <u>will be</u> there about 2:30.

5. The teacher <u>has been waiting</u> for his son.

조동사 (Modal Auxiliary)

의미: 조동사는 단어 특성에 따라 의미가 다양하다.

역할: 문장에서, 주가 되는 일반 동사의 의미를 확대시키는 역할을 한다.

종류: can/could, will/would, shall/should, may/might. must/have to, ought, need

(1) Can / Could

① 능력 : ~할 수 있다

I can play the piano.(현재) = I am able to play the piano.

I could play the piano.(과거) = I was able to play the piano.

I shall be able to speak English.(미래)

I have been able to speak English.(현재완료)

② 허가 : ~해도 좋다

You can play here.(can = may)

Can I smoke here?

Can I go swimming?

You cannot play here.(금지)(= must not, may not)

You cannot play baseball in the garden.(금지)

③요청이나 제안의 표현

Can you give me a ride home?(집에 좀 태워 주시겠습니까?)

* Could you show me the way to the station?(Can 보다 공손한 표현)

(2) May / Might

① 허가 : ~해도 좋다, ~할 수 있다 (= be allowed to ~, be permitted to ~)

You may go there. ↔ You may not go there.

May I use your phone?

② 현실적 가능성(능력) : ~할 수도 있다(= can)

He may know it. ↔ He may not know it. (그는 아마 모를 것이다)

Anyone may see the difference between the two.

③ 추측 : ~일지 모른다.

He may be ill.(현재)

He may have been ill.(과거)

④ 기원문

May you be happy!

May he rest in peace!

(3) Must / Have to

"Must"

① 필요/의무 : ~해야 한다

You must do as you are told.(=have to)

You must put on these clothes.(=have to)

② 강한 추측 : ~임에 틀림없다, 반드시 ~일 것이다

He must be ill. ↔ He cannot be ill. (현재)

He must have been ill. ↔ He cannot have been ill. (과거)

(4) Will / Shall

① 화자(speaker)의 의지

He shall die.(= I will kill him)

You shall have it.(= I will give it to you)

My son shall bring the money to you.

    (= I will let my son bring the money to you)

② 청자(hearer)의 의지

Shall my daughter go first ?

    (= Do you want me to let my daughter go first ?)

Shall he come again ?

    (= Will you let him come again ?)

Will you lend me the book ?

③ 주어의 의지 : 인칭에 관계없이 모두 will을 써서, 의지/고집/주장을 나타낸다.

I will do as I like.

Do what you will.

I shall be very glad if you will help me.

She said, "I will leave here."

(5) Would

① 단순/의지 미래의 과거형

He said that he would pay back.

② will 보다 공손한 표현이나 초대, 권유를 나타낸다.

Would you mind opening the door? (공손한 표현)

Would you like some coffee? (권유)

③ 과거의 습관적 행동

He would sit for hours without saying a word.(습관적 행동)

He would often come back drunk, and beat his wife.(습관적 행동)

(6) Should

① 의무/당연 : 이 때 'should'는 'must' 보다 '의무/당연'의 의미가 약해서 '권고' 또는
'타당함'의 의미를 가지며, had better와 같은 뜻으로 쓰이지만, 그 강도가
'had better'보다 약하다.

Children should obey their parents.(should = ought to)

The young should respect the old.(should = ought to)

② 가능성/추측(should = ought to)

It should be fine tomorrow.

He should arrive by the 8:00 train.

They should be there by now, I think.

* 주장/명령/요구/제안/충고/권고/결정의 동사 뒤에 이어지는 절에서 should가 쓰
인다. 이때 should는 해석되지 않으며, 생략되어 쓰이는 것이 일반적이다.

insist/order, command/desire, require, request, demand, ask/propose,
suggest/advise/recommend/decide, determine

I insist that he (should) be sent there.

I propose that the matter (should) be put to the vote at once.

(7) Ought to 의무/당연 (ought to = should)

He ought to obey his parents.

You ought to start at once.

I told him that he ought to look for her.(= must)

(8) Need

① 긍정문에서 항상 본동사로 쓰이며, 명사나 to부정사를 목적어로 가진다.

He needs to go there.

He needs some money.

He needed to go there.

② 부정문과 의문문에서 조동사나 본동사로 쓰인다.

He doesn't need to go there.(본동사)

Does he need to go there?(본동사)

He need not go there.(조동사)

He didn't need to go there.(본동사의 과거시제)

* 다음의 동사들은 문장에서 본래의 뜻은 나타내지 못하고,
문장에서 기능으로만 역할을 할 때가 있으며, 마치 조동사의 역할을 하는 것 같다.

"Do"

① 강조의 조동사: 본동사 앞에 놓여 본동사를 강조한다.

I do think you ought to go there.

I do wish children weren't so noisy.

② 의문문과 부정문에서

Do you know him ?

You did not finish it.

"Have" 완료구문을 만들기 위해 쓰인다.

I have finished the work already.

A new highway has been built.

"Be" 진행형이나 수동태 구문에서 조동사로 쓰인다.

The president is delivering a speech.

Two large pizzas were delivered.

A. 아래 문장에서 알맞은 것을 고르세요.

1. Eliot (could/ must) be on vacation this week.

2. He (might, have to) meet me at the theater.

3. The boy (can, could) attend the English class in the evening.

4. You (could, should) do obey your parents.

5. They insist that he (should, will) be sent there.

6. (May, Must) I borrow your pen?

7. (Can, Will) I ask you a question?

8. (May, Shall) we dance?

9. (Would, Should) you help me?

10. (Could, May) you be quite. please.

관사
(Article)

관사 (Article)

의미: 형용사에 포함되어 있으며,

그 뜻은 기본적으로 "하나의"(a/an) 혹은 "그" (the)로 나타낸다.

역할: 항상 명사 앞에 쓰이며, 그 명사를 한정한다.

종류는 부정관사 "a/an"과 정관사 "the"가 있다.

(1) 부정관사 "a/an"

① one의 약한 뜻으로 보통 해석하지 않는다.

She is an honest girl.

He is a smart boy.

② "하나"(one의 강한 뜻)

He will finish it in a day or two.

Rome was not built in a day.

Please give me an apple.

③ the same

They are of an age.

Birds of a feather flock together.

of a size(크기가 같은) / of a mind(마음이 맞는) / of a humor(기질이 같은)

④ per(~에, ~마다)

We take three meals a day.

I write to her once a month.

This cloth is 1000 won a yard.

⑤ any (어떤 ~라도, 모든) : 대표단수

A dog is a faithful animal.

A horse is a useful animal.

⑥ a certain(어떤)의 뜻

A Mr. Jones came to see you.

⑦ some(어느 정도, 약간)의 뜻

He was speechless for a time.(얼마 동안, 당분간)

Oil paintings look better at a distance.(거리를 두고)

(2) 정관사 "the"

① 앞에 나온 명사를 반복할 경우

The other day I met a boy. The boy was flying a kite.

He lost a purse, and the purse was found in the garbage.

② 전후관계로 명백히 알 수 있는 경우

Open the door, please.

The post office is near the school.

③ 수식어귀(형용사구, 형용사절)에 의해서 뒤에서 한정될 때 : 특정한 것

The principal of our school is Mr. Han.

The water of this well is not good to drink.

She is the girl whom I met yesterday.

④ 유일한 것

The moon is the satellite of the earth.

He traveled around the world.

⑤ 종족 전체를 나타낼 때(대표단수)

The dog is a faithful animal.

The horse is a useful animal.

⑥ 서수, 최상급, only, same 앞에서 쓰인다.

I took the first train.

He is the tallest boy in our class.

You are the only student who can do it.

I have the same sharp-pencil as you have.

⑦ 시간, 수량의 단위를 나타낼 때 : by + the + 명사(~로, ~당)

He is paid by the day(week, month).

She rented the apartment by the month.

Sugar is sold by the pound.

Cloth is sold by the yard.

⑧ 신체의 일부분을 표시할 때 catch, take, hold + 사람(목적격) + by the 신체일부

He caught me by the neck.[by the arm / by the hand]

⑨ 강, 바다, 해협 등의 이름 앞에

the Thames, the Han River / the Pacific, the Atlantic, the East Sea /

the English Channel, the Straits of Korea, the Magellan Strait.

⑩ 산맥, 군도, 반도의 이름 앞에

the Alps, the Rocky Mountains / the Philippines, the West Indies /

the Korean Peninsula

(3) 관사의 생략

① 일반적 의미의 불가산 명사 및 복수 명사 앞에는 관사를 쓰지 않는다.

Water must be pure if it is to be drunk.

Museums are closed on Monday.

② 호격일 경우
Waiter, give me a cup of coffee.

Father, may I go out?

③ 가족관계일 경우
Mother goes to market in the afternoon.

Father is out, but mother is in.

④ 관직, 신분을 나타내는 말이 동격 또는 보어로 쓰일 때
Elizabeth I, Queen of England, was a great monarch.

They elected him mayor of the city.

He was appointed principal.

⑤ 명사(건물)가 본래의 목적으로 사용될 때
She goes to church every Sunday.

She goes to the church to see her.

He goes to school every day.

He goes to the school to play baseball.

The man went to prison.(투옥되다)

His wife went to the prison to see him.

⑥ 식사, 운동, 학과, 질병이름 앞에
We eat breakfast at seven.

He came immediately after dinner.

He plays tennis every Sunday.

He specializes in mathematics.

He died of cancer.

⑦ 교통수단

by plane[air](=on a plane) / by train(=on a train) / by ship(=on a ship) /
by car(=in a car) / by bus(=on a bus) / by sea(해로로) /
on horseback by coach(마차로) / on foot

⑧ 통신수단

by telephone / by wireless(무선으로) /
by radio(무전으로) by telegram(전보로)

A. 밑줄 친 단어 앞에 관사가 필요하면 써 넣으세요.

1. A Dog is <u>faithful</u> animal.

2. I need to <u>teacher</u> to help me.

3. I think she is <u>music</u> dancer.

4. <u>Water</u> is very important.

5. One of my friends lives in <u>Seoul</u>.

6. We should know <u>life</u> is not so long.

B. 밑줄 친 부정관사의 의미를 보기에서 찾아 쓰세요.

보기) one, per, a certain

1. They talked about a movie. _____

2. There is an apple on the table. _____

3. My son usually drink two glasses of milk a day. _____

C. 빈 칸에 알맞은 관사를 써 넣으세요.

1. (   ) caw is a useful animal

2. I don't have (   ) driver's license.

3. Yesterday, I bought an USB, but I lost (   ) USB.

4. Please, open (   ) door.

5. (   ) sun rises in the east.

6. He caught me by (   ) hand.

Lesson 7

형용사
(Adjective)

형용사(Adjective)

의미: 성질이나 상태를 나타냄

역할: 문장에서 명사를 바로 꾸며주거나, 명사를 보충 설명 해 주는 역할을 한다.

(1) 형용사의 용법

① **한정용법** : 형용사가 명사의 앞 또는 뒤에서 직접 수식하는 것을 말한다.

She is a smart student.

I found an empty box.

② **서술용법** : 형용사가 주어나 목적어를 풀이해 주는 역할을 한다.

　　　즉, 주격보어나 목적격보어로 쓰인다.

The baby is very pretty.

I found him honest.

(2) 형용사의 위치

① **형용사의 어순** : 여러 개의 형용사가 올 경우는 대개 다음의 순서를 따른다.

한정사+수량(서수/기수)+대소+성상+색+신구/노소+재료/소속/기원

Look at the two large fine old stone houses.

She is a tall thin French lady.

* 한정사 : 소유격, 관사, 대명형용사, 부정형용사(some, any, no, little, few, etc.)

② '-thing', '-body'를 수식하는 형용사는 뒤에서 수식한다.

Please give me something cold to drink.

He is a somebody important.

(3) 형용사의 명사 표현

① the + 형용사 : 복수보통명사

The rich stayed the famous hotel.

예) the rich = rich people the poor = poor people

the young = young people the wise = wise people

② the + 형용사 : 추상명사

The woman has an eye the beautiful.

예) the true = truth /the good = good(善) /the beautiful = beauty(美)

(4) 수사

① 기수

one, hundred, thousand, million, billion

* dozen, score, hundred, thousand, million 은 복수수사 다음에 쓰여도 's'를 쓰지 않는다.

예) three score, two hundred, five million

* 막연히 많은 숫자를 나타낼 때는 복수형을 쓴다.

예) dozens of people / scores of students / hundreds of people / thousands of people / millions of people

② 서수 : first, second, third, fifth, eighth, ninth, tenth.

③ 분수 : 분자는 기수로 분모는 서수로 읽으며, 분자를 먼저 읽고 분모를 읽으며, 분자가 복수일 때는 분모의 서수를 복수형(-s)으로 해주어야 한다.

예) ½ a half or one half , ⅓ one third or a third, ⅔ two thirds

¼ one fourth or a quarter

134/200 one hundred (and) thirty four over two hundred

④ 소수 : 소수점은 point로 읽고, 소수점 뒤의 숫자는 하나씩 따로 읽는다.

1.23 one point two three

0.23 zero point two three

13.704 thirteen point seven zero four

⑤ 배 수사 : once, twice, three times, ten times

This is as large as that.

He has twice the number of my books.

This is three times as large as that.

This is three times the size of that.

⑥ 연도 등

1991 : nineteen ninety-one

1990's : nineteen nineties

387~6077 : three eight seven six o double seven

(5) 수량형용사

① Many (수) : 많은, + 셀 수 있는 명사

Many students have repeated the same mistakes.

* as many : 동수의

He made ten mistakes in as many lines.

There were five accidents in as many days.

② Much (양) : 많은, + 셀 수 없는 명사

I have much money.

* as much : 동량의

I thought as much.(그 만큼은, 그 정도는)

He drank two bottles of beer and as much wine.

③ Few (수): 조금, + 셀 수 있는 명사 few (거의 없는 : 부정) a few (조금 있는: 긍정)

He has few friends.

He has a few friends.

④ Little (양): 조금, + 셀 수 없는 명사 little (거의 없는 : 부정) a little(조금 있는: 긍정)

I have little money with me.

I have a little money with me.

A. 밑줄 친 형용사가 꾸며주는 명사를 고르세요.

1. I was late at the meeting because of <u>heavy</u> traffic.
2. Something <u>spicy</u> was put into her soup.
3. There is a ugly <u>broken</u> car on the street.
4. I met somebody <u>famous</u> at the mall.
5. My <u>favorite</u> sport is baseball.

B. 밑줄 친 형용사가 설명해 주고 있는 단어(명사 또는 대명사) 또는 구를 고르세요.

1. The city is <u>fantastic</u>.
2. My mother always made me <u>happy</u>.
3. I know he is very <u>smart.</u>
4. I think they believed him <u>honest</u>.

C. 문장에 알맞은 것을 고르세요.

1. I have (a few, a little) breakfast in the morning.
2. He spent (many, much) days doing his project.
3. There is (many, much) snow in this winter.
4. How (many, much) pictures did you take in USA.
5. I don't have (a few, a little) knowledge about it.
6. The man want to get (a few, a little) notebooks.

부사
(Adverb)

부사(Adverb)

의미: 성질, 상태, 동작, 문장 등의 의미를 보다 분명하게 함

역할: 문장에서 동사, 형용사, 부사 또는 문장 전체를 수식한다.

시간, 장소, 방법, 정도, 빈도 등을 나타낸다.

(1) 부사의 기능

① 동사수식

He speaks English well.

He did not die happily.

② 형용사수식

She is very clever.

This is too expensive.

③ 부사수식

They lived very happily.

④ 문장전체수식

Happily he did not die.

Unfortunately he died.

Probably he will succeed this time.

(2) 부사 형태

① 형용사에다가 'ly'를 붙인다.

slow - slowly / careful - carefully / glad - gladly

② 형용사와 같은 형태의 부사 : early, long, hard, enough, fast, pretty, late, high
　　　　　　　　　　　 등은 형용사와 부사의 형태가 같다.

The early bird catches the worm.

I get up early in the morning.

She wrote a long letter to her teacher.

He was long ill.

He has money enough for his trip.

She is old enough to love.

He is fast runner.

He eats fast.

③ 형용사와 같은 형태의 부사와 -ly 형의 부사가 뜻이 서로 다른 경우가 있다.

It is hard to understand.(어려운)

He studies hard.(열심히)

He hardly studies.(거의 않는)

I was late for school today.

The doctor came too late.

I haven't seen him lately.

She is pretty.(귀여운)

He is pretty well now.(상당히, 꽤)

She is prettily dressed.(예쁘게)

Mt. Baegdu is very high.

The cat can jump high.

It is a highly interesting movie.(굉장히)

(2) 부사의 위치

① 빈도부사의 위치
종류 : always, never, often, sometimes, seldom, rarely, scarcely, regularly,
ever, usually

위치: 빈도부사 + 일반 동사

be 동사 + 빈도부사

조동사 + 빈도부사 + 본동사

He is always at home.

I have never been to England.

I can scarcely understand his words.

It seldom snows in Busan.

* 여러 개의 낱말로 이루어진 구 형태의 빈도부사는 문미나 문두에 위치한다.

now and then, from time to time, on occasion, all the time, twice a week,

now and again, every two days

I go to the language school every two days.

② 장소 + 방법 + 시간
시간부사어구 : 작은 단위 + 큰 단위

장소부사어구 : 좁은 장소 + 넓은 장소

일반부사(구) : 짧은 부사(구) + 긴 부사(구)

I'll visit you at seven o'clock next Sunday.

We arrived safely at the station.

He arrived there safely yesterday.

We lived there happily before.

I met him at the station at five o'clock.

(3) 주의해야 할 부사의 용법

① enough: 일반적으로 부사가 형용사, 부사를 수식할 때는 형용사 앞에 놓이는 것이
　　　　원칙이지만, enough는 수식하는 말 뒤에 놓인다.

He does not work enough.

He is rich enough to buy the Volvo.

② only : 관계가 가장 밀접한 것과 가까이 두는 것이 원칙이다.

Only I can see him in the room.

I can only see him in the room.

I can see only him in the room.

I can see him only in the room.

③ **already 와 yet**

already는 긍정문에 사용: 이미, 벌써

Linda has already gone to bed.

Has the bell rung already ?

yet은 의문문, 부정문에 사용

Has the bell rung yet? (벌써, 이미)

The work is not yet finished. (아직)

* 긍정문에 yet가 사용되면 : 아직, 여전히

She is talking yet.

④ **ago 와 before**

ago: 현재를 기준으로 하여 "지금부터 ~ 전"의 뜻. 항상 과거시제에 사용

before: 과거를 기준으로 하여 "그때부터 ~전"의 뜻. 주로 과거완료에 사용

My father died ten years ago.

I had received a letter three days (ago, before).

When I met him two years ago, he said his son had died five years before.

⑤ 유도부사 there : 문두에서 동사를 이끄는 역할을 한다.

There is a book .

There is no one there.

There used be a bridge here.

There seems to have been a fire.

A. 밑줄 친 부사가 꾸며주는 것을 찾으세요.

1. The doctor talks <u>very</u> fast.

2. <u>Unfortunately</u>, he was absent.

3. He is old <u>enough</u> to take a trip by himself.

4. I slept <u>deeply</u> yesterday.

5. My son learns language <u>quickly</u>.

B. 주어진 부사(구)를 문장에 알맞게 써 넣으세요.

1. She gets up early in the morning, (usually)

2. He is rich to buy the car. (enough)

3. Tom can speak English. (well)

4. I used to go shopping with my husband. (all the time)

5. I am happy to meet you. (really)

C. 밑줄 친 단어의 뜻을 쓰세요.

1. The bus arrived ten minutes <u>late</u>.

2. I haven't seen him <u>lately</u>.

3. The man is working <u>hard.</u>

4. He <u>hardly</u> ever go to church.

5. The cat can jump <u>high.</u>

6. It is a <u>highly</u> interesting movie.

접속사(Conjunction)
전치사(Preposition)

접속사(Conjunction)

의미: 같은 단위를 연결

역할: 단어와 단어, 구와 구, 절과 절을 연결한다.

(1) 등위접속사

① 완전등위 접속사 : 완전히 대등한 단문이나 구를 연결시키는 접속사를 말한다.

ⓐ "and"

- 단일 개념을 나타낸다.

Time and tide wait(s) for no man.

Slow and steady wins the race.

Bread and butter is my favorite breakfast.

- 부정사 대신에 쓰는 경우 : go, come, try, send, run, mind, write 등의 다음에 오는 and는 to 부정사의 대용으로 쓰여 '목적(~하기 위해서)'의 의미를 가진다.

Come and see me.(= Come to see me)

Try and use plain words.(= Try to use plain words)

-명령문 + and : ~하라, 그러면

Work hard, and you will succeed.

Push the button, and the door will open.

ⓑ "but"

Excuse me, but what is your name ?

ⓒ "or"

- or : 말하자면, 즉(= that is, that is to say)

I weigh 110 pounds or about 50 kilograms.

- 명령문 + or = unless, if ~ not (~하라, 그렇지 않으면)

Work hard, or you will fail.(= Unless you work hard, you will fail.)

② 등위 상관접속사

Either you or I am to blame.(A 또는 B 둘 중의 하나)

He can neither ski nor swim.(A와 B 둘 다 아닌)

Both butter and cheese are nutritious foods.(A 와 B 둘 다)

* not only A but (also) B = B as well as A(A 뿐만 아니라 B 역시)

Not only you but also I was wrong. = You as well as I are wrong.

Not money but wisdom is what I want.(A가 아니고 B 인)

(2) 종속접속사

① 명사절을 이끄는 접속사

ⓐ "That" : 주로 단정적인 내용을 이끈다.
- 주절, 목적절, 주격보어절을 이끈다.

That he has gone is certain.(주절)

I think it a pity that you didn't try harder.(목적절)

The trouble is that we are short of money.(주격보어절)

ⓑ "whether" : '~인지 어떤지(아닌지)'의 의미로 양자택일을 요하는 문장을 이끈다.
- 주절을 유도

It is very doubtful whether he will consent (or not).(진주어절)

Whether he is wise or stupid is not important problem.

- 목적절을 유도(whether = if)

I wonder whether the news is true.

I don't know whether he is at home or at the office.

I am not sure whether he will pass the final test (or not).

② 부사절을 이끄는 접속사

- 시간의 부사절을 이끄는 접속사

　　ⓐ " when / as / whenever "

　　· When her husband had an accident, she was coming home for work.

　　· Give her this letter when she comes.(~할 때에, ~하면(= if))

　　· They were about to start fighting when their father intervened.(바로 그때)

　　· He came up as she was speaking.(~할 때(= when))

　　· Whenever I felt lonely, I used to visit his house.(~할 때는 언제나)

　　ⓑ "until" ~할 때까지

　　We stayed there until we finished our work.

　　ⓒ " before" 긍정문 + before : ~해서야(지나서야) 비로소 -하다

　　It will be long before he notices it.(한참 지나서야 그가 알게 될 것이다)

　　It was five years before I met Jane again.

　　　　　(5년이 지나서야 비로소 Jane을 다시 만났다)

　　ⓓ "after"

　　I'll go after I finish my work.

　　ⓔ "since": ~이후로, ~이래로

　　Five years have passed since his father died.

　　He came to New York two years ago and has lived here ever since.

- 이유/원인의 부사절을 이끄는 접속사

　　ⓐ "because" : 직접적인 이유/원인을 나타낸다.

　　He could finish the work because he worked hard.

　　I did not go because I wanted to.(내가 원해서 간 것은 아니었다)

　　ⓑ "since" : because보다 의미가 약하며, 간접적인 이유/원인을 나타낸다.

　　Since no one agrees to my proposal, I will give it up.

ⓒ "for" : because보다 의미가 약하며, comma 뒤에 쓰여서 추가[보충]적 이유/원인을 설명한다.

She was sleeping, for she worked all day.(for=because)

ⓓ "as" : since보다 의미가 약하며, 간접적인 이유/원인을 나타낸다.

As it was cold yesterday, I stayed home all day.

- 목적의 부사절을 이끄는 접속사

(so) that ~ may[can] = in order that ~ may[can] : ~하기 위하여

He worked hard so that he might succeed.
I packed her some food (so) that he wouldn't get hungry.

- 결과의 부사절을 이끄는 접속사

so + 형용사/부사 + that ~ / such + a(an) + 형용사 + 명사 + that ~ : 너무 -해서 ~하다

It was so hot that we went swimming.
It was such a nice weather that we went out for a walk.

- 양보의 부사절을 이끄는 접속사

ⓐ though = although = even though
Though he is poor, he is happy.[although 보다는 구어적인 의미를 가짐]
Even though I don't love her, I have to marry her.(비록 ~라 하더라도)

ⓑ if / even if
If he is poor, he is a nice guy.
Even if we are not rich, we have good friends.

- 장소의 부사절을 이끄는 접속사 (where / wherever)
God knows where he comes from.

Go whereve3u want to go.

- 양태의 부사절을 이끄는 접속사

ⓐ as : ~처럼, ~대로

Do in Rome as the Romans do.

As you treat me, so will I treat you.

ⓑ as if / as though : 마치 ~처럼

He talks as if he knew everything.

- 조건을 이끄는 접속사 (if)

If it's cold tomorrow, I will stay at home.

A. 문장에서 접속사가 연결하고 있는 것에 밑 줄 치세요.

1. I want to buy apples <u>and</u> tomatoes at the shop.

2. We should take this bus <u>or</u> wait for next one.

3. Tom lost his wallet, <u>but</u> his wife found it at the park.

4. To be <u>or</u> not to be, that is a question.

B. 빈칸에 알맞은 단어를 써 넣으세요.

1. (   ) she (   ) I were satisfied with the result.

2. (   ) John or Jane will be a first player.

C. 접속사가 이끄는 절에 밑줄을 치세요.

1. He told me <u>that</u> he couldn't take the position.

2. My wife asked <u>if</u> I wanted to have lunch at home.

3. Mike thought <u>that</u> I had made a mistake.

4. I wonder <u>whether</u> Linda told a lie.

5. <u>That</u> she is honest is clear.

전치사(Preposition)

의미: 다른 품사 단어, 구, 절 앞에 놓여, 그 의미를 나타냄

(1) 전치사의 목적어: 전치사 뒤에 나오는 단어, 구, 절 등을 전치사의 목적어라 한다.

전치사의 목적어로는 명사, 대명사, 형용사, 과거분사, 부사, 동명사, 부정사, 구, 절이 올 수 있다.

① 명사, 대명사

He goes to school by bus.

He lives with Tom.

Let's play with them.

I bought a pencil for him.

* 전치사의 목적어로 대명사가 올 때는 반드시 목적격을 써주어야 한다.

② 형용사, 과거분사, 부사

Things went from bad to worse.

You should not take your parent's sacrifice for granted.

He returned from abroad.

It is far from here.

③ 동명사, 부정사

He is fond of driving in the country.

He is afraid of going alone.

There is nothing but to wait.

I was about to leave.

④ 구

He appeared from behind the tree.

He read the book till late at night.

⑤ 절

From where I was sitting I could not see them.

He will not work except when he is pleased.

(2) 전치사의 종류

① 장소를 나타내는 전치사

at : 비교적 좁은 장소에 사용.

in : 넓은 장소에 사용.

I live at Chongro in Seoul.

He is standing at the door.

I was staying at a hotel in New York.

on : 접촉하여 "위에" / above : 막연한 "위로"(보다 높이)

beneath : 접촉하여 "아래에" / below : 막연한 "아래로"(보다 아래로)

over : 수직으로 바로 "위에" / up : 밑에서 "위(쪽으)로"

under : 수직으로 바로 "아래에" / down : 위에서 "아래(쪽으)로"

There is a vase on the table.

The ice gave way beneath our feet.

The moon has risen above the horizon.

The sun has just sunk below the horizon.

A jet plane flew over the city.

He was lying under the tree.

They went up and down the street.

We sailed down the river.

between : 둘 사이에

among : 셋 이상 사이에

There is a river between the two villages.

Many birds are singing among the trees.

behind : ~의 뒤에   · Who is the man behind the tree ?

after : 뒤를 쫓아   · The dog ran after the rabbit.

in : ~의 안에   · I study in this room.

into : ~의 안으로   · He came into the room.

out of : ~의 밖으로   · He came out of the room.

across : ~을 가로질러, ~을 횡단하여

through : ~을 통과하여

along : ~에 연하여, ~을 따라서

He came across the street.

The train passed through the tunnel.

We walked along the river.

round : ~의 주위에(주위를 도는 운동 상태)

around : ~의 주위에(주위에 정지한 상태)

about : ~의 주위에(막연한 주변, 여기저기)

The earth moves round the sun.

We sat around the bonfire.

He walked about the park.

to : ~로(도착지점을 표시)

for : ~방향으로(행선지나 목적지를 표시)

from : ~에서(출발지점을 표시)

toward : ~의 방향으로(막연한 목표를 표시)

He has gone to England.

He left Seoul for L.A.

The train is for Busan.

He started from Seoul

He bowed toward England.

② '때'를 나타내는 전치사

at : 시각이나 시점 등 짧은 시간을 나타낸다(몇 시, 몇 분, 밤, 정오, 새벽)

on : 일정한 날짜, 요일, 정해진 시간의 아침, 오전, 오후를 나타낸다.

in : at 보다 긴 시간을 나타낸다(년, 월, 계절, 세기, 아침, 저녁, 오후)

at six, at night, at noon, at dawn(= daybreak), at midnight.

on Sunday, on New Year's Day, on May 10th, on the morning of 11th

in April, in Autumn, in 1945, in the 20th Century

till : "~까지"(어느 때까지의 동작의 계속을 나타낸다)

by : "~까지"(어느 때까지의 동작의 완료를 나타낸다)

before : "전에"(어느 때 이전에 동작의 완료를 나타낸다)

I will stay here till five.

I will come here by five.

I will be at that restaurant till you come.

I will finish my work by five.

I usually finish work before six.

in : "~이 지나면"(시간의 경과를 나타낸다. 미래시제가 중심임)

within : "~이내에"(일정한 기간이내를 나타낸다)

after : "~후에"(과거부터)

> She will be back in a few days.
>
> Cancer will kill him in a few weeks.
>
> He will come back within a couple of days.
>
> He came back after few days.

③ 원인/이유의 전치사

for : ~ 때문에

> The boss will blame you for neglecting your job.

from : 직접적인 원인(피로, 부상, 과로등에 의한)

of : 행위의 원인(~으로 : 사망, 병)

> He fell ill from drinking too much.
>
> He died from overwork.

④ 원료/재료의 전치사

of : "~으로 만들어 지다"[물리적 변화 – 형태는 변해도 질은 변하지 않는 경우]

from : "~으로 만들어 지다[화학적 변화 – 형태와 질이 모두 변하는 경우]

in : 표현방법. 수단. 재료

> The bridge is built of wood.
>
> The house was made of wood.
>
> Wine is made from grapes.
>
> Beer is made from barley.
>
> This picture is painted in oils.
>
> You must write letters in ink.

Speak in English.

Look at the woman in white.

⑤ 수단/도구의 전치사

by : "~에 의해서"(행위자). "~을 타고"(운송수단)

with : "~을 가지고, ~으로"(도구)

through : "~을 통하여"(중개, 매개수단)

The novel was written by Hemingway

He traveled by train.

He cut bread with knife.

Write it with a pen.

I looked at the moon through a telescope.

We get knowledge through books.

A. 문장에서 전치사와 한 묶음이 되는 것에 밑줄을 치세요.

1. The USB <u>in</u> the box is expensive.

2. She went <u>to</u> the post office.

3. They usually play soccer <u>at</u> the school.

4. I haven't seen my son <u>in</u> one year.

B. 빈 칸에 알맞은 전치사를 써 넣으세요.

1. I don't have a pen to write (　　　　).

2. Candy is (　　　) Austria

3. He will meet me (　　　　) Sunday.

4. I will be back (　　　　) five o'clock.

5. There are a lot of books (　　　　) the desk.

6. The police station is (　　　　) the corner of the street.

7. The chair is made (　　　　) wood.

부정사
(Infinitive)

부정사(Infinitive)

의미: 동사의 뜻을 그대로 가지고 있으며, 문장에서 다른 품사처럼 쓰인다.

역할: 문장에서 명사, 형용사, 부사처럼 쓰인다.

형태: to + 동사원형

부정사 부정: 부정사 바로 앞에 부정어를 둔다.

(1) 명사적 용법

① 주어의 역할

To live long is the desire of all men.

To know oneself is difficult.

To work hard is the best way to success.

② 목적어의 역할(타동사의)

He promised to go there.

He promised me to return at there.

She wants to study English.

③ 보어의 역할

To live is to suffer.(주격보어)

To see her is to love her.

Our wish is to preserve peace.

You have to persuade him to help the poor child.(목적격보어)

She allowed me to play with it.

We all expected him to come here.

④ 명사구(의문사 + to 부정사)

I don't know where to go.

I don't know when to do it.

I don't know whom to go with.

I wondered how to contact them.

⑤ 진주어/진목적어로서

To make ourselves understood is not easy.

　　　　→ It is not easy to make ourselves understood.

To work hard is the best way to success.

　　　　→ It is the best way to success to work hard.

I make to get up at six every morning a rule.

　　　　→ I make it a rule to get up at six every morning.

⑥ 동격

His ambition, to be a pilot, was never fulfilled.

He has one aim, to make money.

(2) 형용사적 용법

① 한정적 용법

I have no friend to help me.

He is not a person to break his promise.

He is the very man to do this work.

I have no family to look after me.

I bought a book to read on the plane.

There is no time to lose now.

I have a letters to write.

He has many children to look after.

② 서술적 용법(보어역할)

He seems to be honest.(주격보어)

He appears to be honest.(주격보어)

I chanced to meet her in my walk.(주격보어)

I knew him to be diligent.

I told him to do his best.

* "be + to 원형동사"의 용법 : 이때 'to + 원형동사'는 보어가 된다.

ⓐ 예정(~할 예정이다 = be due to, be scheduled to)

We are to meet him here.

The meeting is to be held tomorrow.

He is to make a speech next Monday.

ⓑ 의무/명령(~해야 한다.)

You are to start at once.

You are to obey the law.

ⓒ 가능(~할 수 있다) : 주로 부정문이나 수동태에 사용된다.

Nothing was to be seen.

My house is to be seen from the station.

ⓓ 운명(~할 운명이다 = be destined to, be doomed to, be fated to)

The poet was to die y ung.

He was never to see his wife again.

ⓔ 목적/의도(~하고자 하다 = intended to) : 주로 조건절에서 쓰인다.

If you are to succeed, you must work hard.

If you are to catch the train, you had better hurry.

(3) 부사적 용법

① 목적 : 동작의 목적을 나타낸다. "~하기 위해서"의 뜻으로 해석

We eat to live, not live to eat.

He raised his right hand to ask a question.

He works hard to succeed in life.

② 결과 : 동작의 결과를 나타낸다.

He lived to see his great-grandchildren.

He grew up to be a great poet.

He worked hard only to fail.

He left his home, never to return.

③ 원인 : 감정을 나타내는 동사나 형용사 다음에 오는 부정사는 원인을 나타내며, "~하니", "~해서"의 뜻으로 번역된다.

I am very glad to see you.

I feel sorry to hear of his failure.

He was happy to see his wife again.

I was surprised to find him dead.

She wept to see the sight.

④ 이유, 판단의 근거 : "~을 보니", "~을 하다니"로 해석

He is a happy man to have such a good son.

He must be a fool to say such a thing.

He cannot be rich to ask you for some money.

What a foolish he is to believe such a thing !

How foolish I was to trust him!

⑤ 조건: "만일 ~이면"

To hear him speak English, one would take him for an American.

I should be glad to go with you.

⑥ 양보 : "~할지라도", "비록 ~하여도"

To see it, you would not believe it.

To do his best, he could not succeed in it.

(4) 원형부정사("to"가 없이 동사원형만 쓰는 경우)

① 사역동사 다음에 원형부정사가 쓰인다. 이 때 원형부정사는 목적보어가 된다.

종류 : have, make, let, (help)

Father made me turn off the radio.

I will have him wash the car.

He made me do it.

He let her attend the party.

I will help you (to) do the work. (영국식에서는 to를 쓰기도 한다)

② 지각동사 다음에도 원형부정사가 쓰인다. 이 때 원형 부정사는 목적보어가 된다.

종류 : see, hear, feel, watch, listen to, smell

I heard her play the piano in the concert.

I saw him enter the house.

I did not notice him go upstairs.

They observed the birds come back to their nests one by one.

They listened to me speak.

I felt myself tremble with the cold.

(5) 부정사의 의미상의 주어

① 주어가 부정사의 의미상의 주어인 경우

I expect to pass the examination.

He longed to get the prize.

I want to read this novel.

② 목적어가 부정사의 의미상의 주어인 경우

I expect you to pass the examination.

He told me to work hard.

I advise you to stop smoking.

He allowed me to do so.

He proved it to be true.

③ 의미상의 주어가 「일반인」일 때는 명시하지 않는다.

It is not easy (for us) to learn a foreign language.

④ 사람의 성질이나 특징을 나타내는 형용사 다음에 오는 부정사의 의미상의 주어는
'of + 목적어'를 쓴다.

kind, good, generous, nice, foolish, wise, careful, careless, rude, stupid,
silly, polite, bad, cruel.

It is rude of you to speak in that way.

It is very kind of you to say so.

A. 아래 문장에서 부정사를 확인하고, 그 용법(명사, 형용사, 부사)을 표시하세요.

1. To see is very important in life.

2. I don't have time to read the book.

3. He wants to have lunch with him.

4. I don't know what to do.

5. We have to do our best to win the game.

6. I am glad to see you again.

B. 각 문장에서 밑줄 친 부정사의 의미상의 주어를 확인하세요.

1. Tom wanted <u>to see</u> me yesterday.

2. It is very kind of you <u>to say</u> so.

3. It is very hard for him <u>to get up</u> early in the morning.

4. They told me <u>to meet</u> you here.

5. The man stepped aside for the lady <u>to pass</u>.

C. 문장에 알맞은 것을 고르세요.

1. I saw him (to enter, enter) the classroom.

2. It is impossible (for me, of me) to swim in the river.

3. Jane had him (to finish, finish) the computer game.

4. Let me (look at, to look at) the bag.

5. Do you know what (do, to do) next?

동명사
(Gerund)

동명사(Gerund)

의미: 동사의 뜻을 그대로 가지고 있으며, 문장에서 다른 품사처럼 쓰인다.
역할: 문장에서 동사적 성질을 갖고, 명사 역할을 한다.
형태: 동사원형 + ing
동명사 부정: 동명사 바로 앞에 부정어를 둔다.

(1) 동명사의 역할

① 주어

Travelling by car is very interesting.
Seeing is believing.

② 목적어

She began crying bitterly.
I don't like swimming in the river.
She is proud of being a beauty.(전치사의 목적어)
I am fond of swimming.(전치사의 목적어)

③ 보어

My hobby is collecting foreign stamps.
My dream is meeting the poet.
It is throwing your money away.

* 동명사와 현재분사의 구별
　　현재 분사: 상태나 동작을 나타내어 '~ 하고 있는'의 뜻
　　동명사: 목적이나 용도를 나타내며 '~하기 위하여'의 뜻

a sleeping baby = a child who is sleeping

a sleeping car = a car used for sleeping

a waiting lady = a lady who is waiting

a waiting room = a room for waiting

(2) 동명사의 의미상의 주어

의미상의 주어가 문장 주어와 같을 때는 생략하고, 문장주어와 다를 때는 그 의미상의 주어를 써 주어야 한다. 그러나 문장주어와는 다르지만 그 문장의 목적어와 같을 때는 생략한다.

① 문장주어와 동일할 때

I am not ashamed of being poor.

He is proud of being a scholar.

② 문장주어와 다를 때

I insist on his going there.

I insist on my son going there.

(3) 동명사의 시제

동명사의 형태는 단순동명사와 완료동명사로 나뉜다. 단순동명사는 그 시제가 술부의 시제와 같거나 하나 더 나아간 미래의 시제이며, 완료 동명사는 술부의 동사보다 하나 앞선 시제이다.

① 단순동명사

He is proud of being bold.

    = He is proud that he is bold.

He was proud of being bold.

    = He was proud that he was bold.

He is sure of passing the examination.

    = He is sure that he will pass the examination.

② 완료동명사

I regret having been lazy.

    = I regret that I have been(was) lazy.

He regretted having done so.

    = He regretted that he had done so.

I never heard of such a thing having been done.

    = I never heard that such a thing had been done.

(4) 동사에 따른 목적어 형태 (동명사와 부정사)

① 부정사와 동명사 둘 다를 목적어로 취하는 동사
attempt, begin, cease, continue, intend, like, love, omit, start

It continued raining (to rain) all day.

I like taking (to take) a nap after lunch.

I love watching(to watch) T.V.

* 목적어가 동명사 또는 부정사 일 때 의미가 달라지는 경우

stop + 동명사(~하는 것을 멈추다): I stopped smoking.

stop + 부정사(~하기 위해 멈추다): I stopped to smoke.

remember + 동명사(~한 것을 기억하다): I remember meeting him.

remember + 부정사(~할 것을 기억하고 있다): I remember to meet him.

forget + 동명사(~한 것을 잊어버리다): I forgot posting the letter.

forget + 부정사(~할 것을 잊어버리다): I forgot to post the letter.

try + 동명사(시험 삼아 ~하다): He tried moving the piano.

try + 부정사(~하려고 시도하다, 노력하다): He tried to move the piano.

go on + 동명사(계속해서 ~하다): He went on talking about his life.

go on + 부정사(쉬었다가 다시 계속하다): He went on to talk about his life.

② 동명사만을 목적어로 취하는 동사

admit, appreciate, avoid, consider, deny, enjoy, escape, finish, keep, mind, postpone, quit, remind, suggest,

You should quit smoking.

Everyone enjoys singing a song.

She finished reading the novel this morning.

③ 부정사만을 목적어로 취하는 동사

agree, appear, ask, choose, decide, demand, desire, expect, hope, learn, manage, plan, pretend. promise, propose, refuse, seem, tend, want, wish

He promised me not to tell a lie.

He decided to study hard.

I expect to be promoted to manager soon.

(5) 동명사의 관용적 용법

It is no use ~ing = It is of no use + to 부정사 : "~해도 소용없다"

It is no use crying over spilt milk.

= It is of no use to cry over spilt milk.

It goes without saying that ~ : "~은 말할 필요조차 없다"

It goes without saying that honesty is the key to success.

cannot help ~ing = cannot but + 원형 : "~하지 않을 수 없다. ~할 수밖에 없다"

I could not help laughing at the funny sight.

= I could not but laugh at the funny sight.

feel like ~ing : "~하고 싶은 생각이 들다"

I feel like making a trip somewhere.

be busy ~ing : "~하는데 분주하다. ~하느라고 바쁘다"
He was busy preparing for the exam.

go ~ing : ~하러 가다(주로 여가 활동을 언급할 때 쓰인다)
I went fishing yesterday.

look forward to ~ing : "~을 기대하다"
I am looking forward to seeing you again.

A. 아래 문장에서 동명사를 확인하고, 그 역할(주어, 보어, 목적어)을 표시하세요.

1. Talking with him is very interesting.

2. The students often avoid answering their teacher's questions.

3. My mother stopped me from making a mistake.

4. Her hobby is gardening.

5. Thanks for inviting me.

B. 아래 문장에서 알맞은 것을 선택하세요.

1. He decided (to buy, buying) the car.

2. All of them don't want (to play, playing) soccer.

3. I don't mind (to study, studying) with him.

4. My brother is busy (to do, doing) his project.

5. We can't help (to laugh, laughing) at his jokes.

6. He promised (to let, letting) me know what the teacher said.

7. Could you show me a (to sleep, sleeping) bag?

분사
(Participle)

분사(Participle)

의미: 동사의 뜻을 그대로 가지고 있으며, 문장에서 다른 품사처럼 쓰인다.

역할: 문장에서 동사적 성질을 갖고, 동사 또는 형용사처럼 쓰인다.

형태: 동사원형 + ing or 동사원형 + ed

종류: 현재분사, 과거분사

* 동사역할: 진행형, 완료형, 수동태에서 쓰일 때

He is studying English.

The book was written by me.

They have worked for five years.

(1) 분사의 의미

① 현재분사 : 진행(~하고 있는), 능동 또는 사역(~시키는, ~하게 하는)을 나타냄

A rolling stone gathers no moss.

People living in the country generally live long.

Look at that falling leaves.

A growing number of young people seek a job.

② 과거분사 : 완료나 상태(~한, ~해버린), 수동(~된, ~당한, ~받은)을 나타냄

Look at the mountain covered with snow.

A wounded soldier lay bleeding.

The broken computer is mine.

* 의미 비교

It was an exiting game.

An exited spectator starts yelling.

He was exited by the news of the victory

The baseball game was exiting.

The story is interesting.

He was interested in the subject.

It is a surprising event.

I was surprised to hear the news.

His speech was boring

I was bored to hear his speech.

(2) 분사의 용법

① 한정적 용법
ⓐ 전위수식: 분사가 단독으로 명사 앞에서 그 명사를 수식한다.

Don't wake up the sleeping child.

Spoken language and written language are two aspects of language.

ⓑ 후위 수식: 분사가 단독으로 쓰이더라도 대명사를 수식할 때.

Those swimming in the pond are my classmates.

Of those invited, all but Tom came to the party.

분사가 보어, 목적어, 부사(구) 등의 부속어구와 같이 쓰이면
형용사구가 되어 후위 수식한다.

The child sleeping there is Mary.

Once there lived a man named Robin Hood.

② 서술적 용법
ⓐ 주격보어로 쓰일 때

He sat reading a novel.

He stood looking at the picture.)

He sat surrounded by his children.

He came in quite exhausted.

ⓑ 목적격보어로 쓰인다.

I saw him going into the room.

I felt myself watched all the time.

I heard him well spoken of.

I couldn't make myself understood in English.

(3) 분사 구문

복문(두개 이상의 절로 만들어진 문장)에서 분사로 시작하는 절에서 사용되며, 사용된 분사는 접속사 + 주어 + 동사가 포함되어 있는 것

① 때 : when, while, as, after.

Walking along the street, I met an old friend of mine.

 → While I was walking along the street, I met an old friend of mine.

Left alone, I began to read.

 → When I was left alone, I began to read.

* 다음의 경우에는 being 과 having been 은 생략되는 것이 보통이다.

ⓐ 분사구문이 수동태일 경우(과거분사 앞에 놓일 때)

As he was wounded in the legs, he could not walk.

 → (Being) Wounded in the legs, he could not work.

As I had been pleased with the article, I bought it.

 → (Having been) Pleased with the article, I bought it.

ⓑ 형용사, 명사, 부사, 현재분사 앞에 놓일 때

(Having been) Lazy all his life, he had nothing to offer to his son.

As he is an expert, he knows how to do it.

 → (Being) An expert, he knows how to do it.

(Being) Only a poor student, I hadn't money enough to buy it.

As I was reading a book, he came in.

→ (Being) Reading a book, he came in.

② 원인, 이유 : as, because, since

Having nothing to do, I went to bed.

→ As I had nothing to do, I went to bed.

Not knowing what to do, he just stood and looked.

→ As he did not know what to do, he just stood and looked.

* 분사구문의 부정 : 분사 앞에 not 또는 never를 붙인다.

③ 조건 : if

Meeting her, I shall be very glad.

→ If I meet her, I shall be very glad.

Read carelessly, Some books will do more harm than good.

→ If they are read carelessly, some books will do more harm than good.

④ 양보 : though, although, even if

Young, she has much experience.

→ Though she is young, she has much experience.

Born of the same parents, they bear no resemblance.

→ Though they were born of the same parents, they bear no resemblance.

⑤ 부대상황

ⓐ 동시동작 : while, as (~하면서)

Smiling brightly, she shook hands with me.

→ She smiled brightly and shook hands with me.

Raising his hands, he stood up and answered.

→ As he raised his hands, he stood up and answered.

Singing and dancing together, we had a good time.

→ As we sang and danced together, we had a good time.

ⓑ 연속동작 : and + 동사 (그리고 ~하다)

We started in the morning, arriving in Seoul at seven.

→We started in the morning, and arrived in Seoul at seven.

He picked up a stone, throwing it at a dog.

→ He picked up a stone, and threw it at a dog.

(4) 분사의 시제

분사는 단순형 분사와 완료형 분사로 나눌 수 있다. 단순형 분사는 주절의 시제와 같은 시제를, 완료형 분사는 주절의 시제보다 하나 앞선 시제를 나타낸다. 즉, 주절의 동사가 현재이면 완료형 분사의 시제는 과거 또는 현재완료이며, 주절의 동사가 과거이면 완료형분사의 시제는 과거완료가 된다.

Living in the country, I am very healthy.

→ As I live in the country, I am very healthy.

Having finished the work, I have much free time now.

→ As I have finished the work, I have much free time now.

Written in plain English, this book is very easy to read.

→ As this book is written in plain English, it is very easy to read.

Scolded, she cried.

→ As she was scolded, she cried.

(5) 독립분사구문

분사구문의 의미상의 주어가 주절의 주어와 다를 경우에는 의미상의 주어를 따로 써 주어야 한다. 이와 같이 분사구문의 의미상의 주어가 주절의 주어와 다른 분사구문을

독립분사구문이라고 한다.

After the sun had set, we gave up looking for them.

    → The sun having set, we gave up looking for them.

As it was fine, we went for a walk.

    → It being fine, we went for a walk.

We shall start tomorrow, if (the) weather permits.

    → We shall start tomorrow, weather permitting.

Though I admit what you say, my friends still don't believe it.

    → I admitting what you say, my friends still don't believe it.

He was reading a book, and his wife was knitting beside him.

    → He was reading a book, his wife knitting beside him.

A. 밑줄 분사가 수식하고 있는 것을 확인하세요.

1. The old man <u>sitting</u> on the bench looks tired.
2. The <u>broken</u> computer will be fixed.
3. I couldn't believe the <u>shocking</u> news.
4. All of the <u>invited</u> students enjoyed the show.
5. The meeting <u>scheduled</u> for this evening is canceled.

B. 문장에 알맞은 형태를 고르세요.

1. She left the door (unlocking, unlocked).
2. The (retiring, retired) man visited the company.
3. They found the (losing, lost) child in the park.
4. The game was very (exciting, excited).
5. The building (painting, painted) green is a shopping center.

C. 밑줄 친 분사를 풀어쓰세요.

1. <u>Seeing</u> me, he ran away.
2. <u>Finishing</u> the homework, she takes a nap.
3. <u>Being</u> sick, Tom didn't attend the meeting.
4. <u>Following</u> this road, you will find the police station.
5. <u>Being</u> sick, I finished the project.

수동태
(Passive)

수동태(Passive)

의미: 의사 전달에 있어 문장주어의 관점에 따른 문장표현 방법으로, 일반적으로 많은 문장들은 능동문으로 사용되고 있으나, 때때로 주어가 동작이나, 행위를 받는 문장을 사용할 때가 있다. 이를 수동태 문장이라 한다.

역할: 주어가 동작을 받는 문장으로서 각종 보고서나 전달문의 문장으로 사용되고, 때때로 강조를 하고자 할 때 사용한다.

일반구조: 주어 + be동사 + 과거분사 + by 목적어

(1) 태의 전환

능동태와 수동태 : 능동태는 동작을 하는 쪽에, 수동태는 동작을 받는 쪽에 중점

① 능동태를 수동태로 바꿀 때
ⓐ 능동태의 목적어가 수동태의 주어가 된다.
ⓑ 능동태의 동사는 be + 과거분사의 형태로 바뀐다.
ⓒ 능동태의 주어는 by + 목적격의 형태로 부사구를 이룬다.

He wrote this letter.
　　→ This letter was written by him.
All the people in the world admire Kennedy.
　　→ Kennedy is admired by all the people in the world.

* 주의 : 자동사는 수동태가 될 수 없다.
lie, sit, rise, die, arrive, work, wait, belong,
consist, (dis)appear, exist, occur, happen, originate,

The cost of transportation has been risen with the price of gasoline.(X)

* 주의 : 타동사이지만 수동태로 전환할 수 없는 동사

resemble, have, meet, lack, escape, belong to, let.

He resembles his father.

   → His father is resembled by him.(X)

He escaped death.

   → Death was escaped by him.(X)

(2) 수동태의 시제 : 수동태의 be 동사는 능동태 동사의 시제와 일치한다.

The hotel was built (by people) in 1994.

	현재	과거	미래
단순형	is built	was built	will be built
완료형	has been built	had been built	will have been built
진행형	is being built	was being built	(will be being built)

* 주의 : 조동사가 있을 경우에 조동사는 그대로 둔다. 그러나 will, shall은 인칭에 맞게 바꾸어 주어야 한다.

You must read the book.

   → The book must be read by you.

Jack can build the house.

   → The house can be built by Jack.

(3) 주의할 수동태

① 4형식의 수동태 : 능동태 4형식에 있는 직접목적어와 간접목적어를 주어로 선택 할 수 있다.

Henry gave me these books.

    → I was given these books by Henry.

      These books were given me by Henry.

      These books were given to me by Henry.

He asked me the question.

    → I was asked the question by him.

      The question was asked me by him.

      The question was asked of me by him.

* 직접 목적어를 주어로 하여 전치사를 수반할 때. 직접 목적어를 주어로 하면 간접 목적어는 보류목적어(Retained Object)가 된다. 이 때 보류목적어 앞에는 to, for, of 등의 전치사가 놓인다.

send, tell, lend, give : to / make, buy : for / ask, require, inquire : of

* 주의: make, buy, write, sing, send, pass, get, bring 등의 수여동사는 직접 목적어만 수동태의 주어가 될 수 있다.

    I wrote him a letter. → A letter was written him by me.(O)

                      He was written a letter by me.(X)

    She sang me a song. → A song was sung me by her.(O)

                    I was sung a song by her.(X)

* 주의 : spare, save, envy, kiss, answer 등의 수여동사는 간접 목적어만 수동태의 주어가 될 수 있다.

    They envied him his luck.

      → He was envied his luck by them.(O)

        His luck was envied him by them.(X)

He kissed her good night.

    → She was kissed good night by him.

② 능동태 5형식을 수동태로 고치면 2형식이 된다. 이 때 막연한 일반인을 나타내는 we, you, one, they, people, somebody, someone 등은 수동태에서 생략되는 경우가 많다.

· I painted the gate green. → The gate was painted green by me.
· They elected Kennedy President.→ Kennedy was elected President.(by them)
· They elected him chairman. → He was elected chairman.(by them)

③ 보어가 원형부정사인 수동태 : 술부동사가 지각동사 또는 사역동사일 경우, 원형 부정사는 수동태에서 "to 부정사"로 바뀐다.

He made me do it.
　　　→ I was made to do it by him.
We saw him enter the room.
　　　→ He was seen to enter the room.(by us)
We heard him sing.
　　　→ He was heard to sing by us.

(4) 의문문의 수동태

① 의문사가 없는 의문문

Did you plant this tree ?

평서문 → You planted this tree.
수동태 → This tree was planted by you.
의문문 → Was this tree planted by you?

② 의문사가 있는 의문문

What did he do ?

평서문 → He did what. (비문장)

수동태 → What was done by him. (비문장)

의문문 → What was done by him ?

(5) 수동태가 많이 쓰이는 경우

① 능동태의 주어가 분명치 않을 때

He was killed in the war.

The continent was discovered about 300 years ago.

② 능동태의 주어가 막연한 일반인을 나타낼 때

Spanish is spoken in Mexico, too.

The rule was seldom observed.

③ 능동태의 주어보다 수동태의 주어에 더 관심이 클 때

The child was run over by a car.

Mr. Reagan was elected President again.

The bed was not slept in.

④ 수동태의 의미가 거의 없이 자동사로 느껴지는 경우

He was drowned while swimming in this river.

Her eyes were drowned in tears.

He was suddenly taken ill.

My University is located on the hill.

He was born in 1970.

He is ashamed of what he did.

(6) 수동태에서 "by" 이외의 전치사를 쓰는 경우

① "at"을 쓰는 동사: surprise, shock

I am surprised at the news.

② "in"을 쓰는 동사: interest

I am interested in the movie.

③ "with"을 쓰는 동사: cover, satisfy, please

I am satisfied with the result.

A. 아래 문장이 능동태문장인지, 수동태 문장인지 확인하세요.

1. Tom bought Jane a ring.

2. The shopping mall will be opened soon.

3. He has waited his children for two hours.

4. Many students has respected the teacher.

5. The book was published.

B. 아래 문장을 수동태로 바꾸세요.

1. They broke the window yesterday.

2. Shakespeare wrote Hamlet.

3. The policeman arrested the thief.

4. I will finish the project.

5. He gave me a gift .

C. 빈 칸에 알맞은 전치사를 쓰세요.

1. I am interested (   ) English.

2. My father satisfied (   ) his work.

3. The ground is covered (   ) snow.

4. He was surprised (   ) the news.

관계사
(Relative)

관계사 (Relative)

의미: 두 문장을 하나로 연결하지만, 순수 접속사와 달리 선행사가 있다.

역할: 접속사 + 명사 혹은 부사 역할

종류: 관계 대명사, 관계부사

(1) 관계대명사

주격	소유격	목적격	선행사
who	whose	whom	**사람**
which	whose/of which	which	**사물/동물**
that	–	that	**사람/사물/동물**
what	–	what	**(선행사 포함)**

① Who

ⓐ 주격

He is the man.＋ He saved the child.

→ He is the man who saved the child.

I employed a man + He I thought was honest.

→ I employed a man who I thought was honest.

ⓑ 소유격

This is the gentleman. + His pulse has been stolen.

→ This is the gentleman whose purse has been stolen.

A child is called an orphan. + His parents are dead.

→ A child whose parents are dead is called an orphan.

ⓒ 목적격

He is the man. + She saved him.

→ He is the man whom she saved.

I employed a man. + I thought him to be honest.

→ I employed a man whom I thought to be honest.

② Which

ⓐ 주격

I have a book + It is very interesting.

→ I have a book which is very interesting.

ⓑ 목적격

This is the book + I bought it yesterday.

→ This is the book which I bought yesterday.

ⓒ 소유격 : whose, of which

The house is my uncle's. + Its roof is red.

→ The house whose roof is red is my uncle's.

→ The house of which the roof is red is my uncle's.

③ That

ⓐ 선행사에 최상급, 서수, the only, the very, the last, the first등과 같은 강한 한정 어구가 붙을 때나, 선행사가 부정형용사(any, no, all, some, little, few, much)에 의해 수식을 받을 때 관계대명사 who 또는 which 보다 that을 주로 쓴다.

This is the best movie that I have ever seen.

He is the only poet that I know well.

There is no man that doesn't love his own country.

ⓑ 선행사가 "사람+동물", "사람+사물"일 때.

Look at the boy and his dog that are running over there.

The driver and the car that fell into the river have not been found.

④ What

선행사를 포함하고 있기 때문에 what = that which, the thing which, all that 등으로 바꿀 수 있다.

ⓐ 주어절 : What I want is your advice. (What = That which)

ⓑ 보어절 : I am not what I used to be.(what = the man that)

ⓒ 목적어절 : I will do what I can. (what = all that)

⑤ 관계대명사의 두 용법 (" , "의 유무에 따라 구분)

ⓐ 제한적 용법

He had two sons who became doctors.

She is the first love that I loved.

ⓑ 계속적 용법 : 관계대명사가 계속적 용법으로 쓰일 때, 문장의 내용에 따라 접속사 + 대명사(and, but, for, though + 대명사)로 바꾸어 쓸 수 있다.

He had two sons, who became doctors.(who = and they)

We trust him, who is very honest.(who = for he)

This book, which is old, is of great value to me.(which = though it)

* 관계대명사 what와 that는 계속적 용법이 없다.

I cannot understand, what he says.(X)

He has a horse, that runs very fast.(X)

⑥ 관계대명사의 생략 (목적격 관계대명사)

ⓐ 동사의 목적어가 될 때

This is the man (whom) I like best.

The movie (which) I saw yesterday was interesting.

He is the only poet (that) I know well.

ⓑ 전치사의 목적어가 될 때

This is the man (whom) you spoke of the other day.

This is the hotel (which) we stopped at last time.

(2) 관계부사

선행사를 가지면서, 접속사와 부사의 구실을 한다. 이 때 선행사 시간(때), 장소, 이유, 방법을 나타내는 명사이다. 관계부사는 전치사 + which로 바꾸어 쓸 수 있다.

종류 : when, where, why, how

① when : 선행사가 time, day, occasion, season 등의 "때"를 나타낼 때 쓰인다. 이 때 when 은 at, in, on, during + which 로 바꾸어 쓸 수 있다.

I don't know the time. + It happened then.

    → I don't know the time when it happened. (when = at which)

② where : 선행사가 place, house, town, village 등의 "장소"를 나타낼 때 쓰인다. 이 때 where 는 in, at, to + which 로 바꾸어 쓸 수 있다.

This is the village. + I was born there.

    → This is the village where I was born. (where = in which)

③ why : 선행사가 reason일 때 쓰인다. why는 for + which로 바꾸어 쓸 수 있다.

Tell me the reason. + You did not come for that reason.

    → Tell me the reason why you did not come.(why = for which)

④ how : 방법을 나타내며, 선행사 없이 쓰인다.

This is the way. + It happened in that way.

→ This is (the way) how it happened.

→ This is the way in which it happened.

(3) 복합관계사

① 복합관계대명사

복합관계대명사는 관계대명사 + ever의 형태로서, 자체에 선행사를 포함하고 있으며(선행사 + 관계대명사), 명사절 또는 부사절로 쓰인다.

종류: whoever, whomever, whosever, whichever, whatever

ⓐ 명사절을 유도할 때

Whoever comes is welcome.(=Anyone who: ~하는 사람은 누구나)

Give it to whomever you like.(=anyone whom)

Return it whosever address is on it.(=anyone whose)

You may take whichever you like.(=anything that: ~하는 것은 어느 것이나)

I will give you whatever you need.(=anything that: ~하는 것은 무엇이나)

ⓑ 양보의 부사절을 유도할 때 : '누가/누구를/어떤 것을/무엇을 ~한다 할지라도'

Whoever may break this law, he will be punished.(= No matter who)

Whomever you may love, he will desert you.(= No matter whom)

Whichever you may choose, you will be interested in it.(= No matter which)

Whatever happens, I will go.(= No matter what)

② 복합관계부사

선행사를 자체에 포함하고 있으며 부사절을 유도한다.

종류:wherever, whenever, however

ⓐ wherever 장소의 부사절 : ~하는 곳은 어디든지
　　　　　양보의 부사절 : ~로(에) ...할지라도

You may go wherever you like. (= at any place where)

Wherever she is, I will find her.(= No matter where)

ⓑ whenever 시간의 부사절 : ~할 때는 언제나
　　　　　양보의 부사절 : 언제 ~할지라도

You may come whenever you like.(= at any time that)

Whenever you may call on me, you will find me at my desk.(= No matter when)

ⓒ however 양보의 부사절 : 아무리 ~할지라도

However hard you may try, you cannot do it in a week.(= No matter how)

However rich a man may be, he should not be idle.(= No matter how)

A. 아래 문장에서 관계사와 선행사에 밑줄을 치세요.

1. I know him who lives in Denver.

2. This is the phone which I bought yesterday.

3. He met a man whose son is a singer.

4. This is the only pen that I have.

5. I don't know the time when the shop is open.

B. 두개의 문장을 하나로 합치세요.

1. This is the book. I want to buy it.

2. This is the town. I was born there.

3. I bought a phone. Its screen is wide.

4. He likes the computer. His father bought him it.

5. I know a man. He works for the company.

C. 빈칸에 알맞은 관계사를 써 넣으세요.

1. Do you know the man (   ) is watching the game?

2. I have a girl friend (   ) father is a professor.

3. I gave my son all the money (   ) I had.

4. Sunday is the day (   ) we go to church.

5. Do you know the reason (   ) he is so happy?

일치
(Agreement)

일치(Agreement)

의미: 영어에서는 주어에 따라서 동사가 단수형인가 복수형인가를 선택하여야 한다.

(1) 주어와 동사의 일치

① 주어의 단수와 복수

My friend lives in Boston.

My brother and sister live in Boston.

② 명사구나 절이 주어가 되는 경우 : 단수로 받는다.

Growing flowers is her hobby. (동명사구)

To live long is the desire of man.(부정사구)

Whether he will agree with me is doubtful.(명사절)

③ and로 연결되는 경우

and로 연결되는 두 개 이상의 명사가 별개의 사람이나 사물이면 복수로, 동일한 사람이나 사물이면 단수로 취급한다.

John and Jim are roommates this semester.

A teacher and scientist is supposed to come.

④ 형용사 every 와 each ⇒ 단수를 수식하고, 단수 취급한다.

Every boy and girl is taught to read and write.

Every man, woman, and child needs love.

Each book and magazine is listed in the card catalog.

(2) 수량 표시

① each[one / every one] of + 복수명사 ⇒ 단수 취급

Every one of my friends is here.

One of the most famous films is Gone with the Wind.

Each of the boys has his own desk.

② a number of + 복수명사 ⇒ 복수 취급

the number of + 복수명사 ⇒ 단수 취급

A number of students were late for class. (a number of = many)

The number of students in the class is fifteen.(~의 숫자)

③ many a + 단수명사 ⇒ 단수 취급

Many a soldier was killed at the field.

(3) 수의 일치

① 'there'로 유도되는 구문의 동사는 주어와 일치시킨다.

There are twenty students in my class.

There's a fly in the room.

② 회사[단체] 이름, 지명, 학문 명, 유희 등은 단수로 받는다.

Sears is a department store.

Physics is easy for her.

Billiards is usually played by two persons.

③ 시간, 거리, 가격의 표현이 하나의 의미로 쓰일 경우 단수취급 한다.

Eight hours of sleep is enough.

Ten years is a long time to wait.

Five thousand miles is too far to travel.

Ten dollars is too much to pay.

④ 수식 표현은 단수 취급한다.

Two and two[Two plus two] is/equals four.

Five times five is twenty five.

Ten minus five leaves/equals five.

Fifteen divided by three is five

⑤ 나라 이름이나 그 나라 언어를 나타낼 때 : 단수

　그 나라 사람들을 나타낼 때 : 복수

English is spoken in many countries.

Chinese is his native language.

The English drink tea.

The Chinese have an interesting history.

The Americans are a passionate people.

The Koreans are a peace-loving people.

⑥ the + 형용사 : 복수보통명사

The rich get richer.(= rich people)

The poor have many problems.(= poor people)

the young(젊은 사람들) / the dead(죽은 사람들)

⑦ 상관 접속사의 일치

ⓐ either A or B / neither A nor B / A or B ⇒ B에 일치(B가 주어)
John or I am to blame.

ⓑ not only A but also B ⇒ B / A as well as B ⇒ A에 일치
James, as well as his friends, was injured in the accident.

ⓒ both A and B ⇒ 복수 취급

Both brother and sister are dead.

⑧ 집합명사(단일성 강조) ⇒ 단수취급 / 군집명사(개별성 강조) ⇒ 복수 취급

My family is large.

All my family are early risers.

The audience was a large one.

The audience were all deeply moved.

⑨ 항상 복수 취급하는 명사

ⓐ police, peasantry, clergy, nobility : 정관사와 같이 쓰인다.

The police are on the murderer's track.

The clergy are all kindness to the poor.

ⓑ people, cattle, poultry : 부정관사도 못 붙이고 복수형으로 쓰이지도 않는다.

Those people are from Canada.

Cattle feed on grass.

⑩ 형식은 복수이지만, 하나의 단위로 취급해서 단수로 받는다.

Ten years is a long time to wait.

A hundred miles is a long distance.

Five hundred dollars a month is a small sum to him.

⑪ It is~that 강조 구문에서는 강조되는 부분과 일치

It is you that are to blame.

It is I who am fit to do this work.

A. 문장에 알맞은 형태를 고르세요.

1. The pen on the desk (is, are) mine.

2. Tom and Bill (live, lives) together in the house.

3. Many a soldier (was, were) killed at the war.

4. There (is, are) many people at the room.

5. Either you or I (am, are) supposed to attend the meeting.

6. My family (is, are) all very well.

7. Every boy and every girl in the room (watch, watches) T.V.

8. The doctor and artist (is, are) my friend.

9. Each of them (is, are) happy.

10. Mathematics (is, are) my favorite subject.

11. Not only she but also I (like, likes) the teacher.

12. Ten dollars (is, are) too much to pay.

Appendix

연습문제 정답
(Answers)

Lesson 1

Picture Description

1. (A) The van is parked.

2. (A) The man is leaning on the booth.

3. (A) They are running together.

4. (B) There is an attendant.

5. (B) They are shopping.

Questions and Responses

1. (B) He deceived me again.

2. (A) About three hours.

3. (B) Your sister called at 3 o'clock.

4. (C) I want to see the stock market.

5. (C) What time would you like?

Short Conversations

1. (B) At a garage.

2. (C) A report typed poorly.

3. (A) To carry the bag.

4. (A) He will relocate the office.

5. (D) She had dropped her keys.

Lesson 2

Picture Description

1. (C) They are rowing the boat.

2. (A) The man is standing in front of several people.

3. (D) Some people are taking a rest on the benches

4. (A) They are standing in a row.

5. (B) There are cars close to the gas station.

Questions and Responses

1. (A) Yes, here you are.

2. (B) There is a big game this Saturday.

3. (A) Just two hours.

4. (A) I got an e-mail yesterday.

5. (B) Yes, you can.

Short Conversations

1. (C) Jack.

2. (B) Wednesday.

3. (B) He is on business.

4. (A) Her weight.

5. (D) They will go to a pet shop.

Lesson 3

Picture Description

1. (D) The bench is by the tree.

2. (C) There are many trees by the road.

3. (B) The baggage is loaded.

4. (A) There are several balconies.

5. (A) They are walking together.

Questions and Responses

1. (C) Yes, please.

2. (B) It's very exciting.

3. (A) Around ten-thirty

4. (B) At our headquarters.

5. (B) Sure. What can I do for you?

Short Conversations

1. (B) Go shopping.

2. (A) He will move to another place.

3. (D) He will go to the store.

4. (D) At a stationery.

5. (D) She is going to promote.

Lesson 4

Picture Description

1. (A) She is reading.

2. (A) They are watching each other.

3. (A) The woman is holding the pole.

4. (B) There are several cars on the road.

5. (A) The train is on the rail.

Questions and Responses

1. (B) Sure

2. (C) Can I have ice cream.

3. (B) You are on Broadway Street.

4. (A) The window is broken.

5. (B) Thank you. I'm listening.

Short Conversations

1. (D) Doctor and patient.

2. (B) A clearance sale.

3. (D) She is trying to get a refund.

4. (A) Something is wrong with the number.

5. (C) 2:30.

Lesson 5

Picture Description

1. (B) The man is looking at the backside.
2. (A) There are many trees in a row.
3. (C) They are across the street.
4. (B) The cars are parked side by side.
5. (A) There are many people under the tree.

Questions and Responses

1. (B) No, thank you. I am full.
2. (B) I am not sure, but I'll try.
3. (B) I went to the new shopping center.
4. (A) Yes, I don't like meat.
5. (C) No, I'll carry my suitcase.

Short Conversations

1. (D) She will call her landlord.
2. (D) A technician.
3. (B) An office building.
4. (C) He wants to sell a used car.
5. (A) She was talking with another person.

Lesson 6

Picture Description

1. (B) The woman is bringing a bag.
2. (A) There is a pot on the table.
3. (C) There are many products on the table.
4. (A) The man is lying under the tree.
5. (B) The car is parked with the motorcycles.

Questions and Responses

1. (A) Yes I'll do it.
2. (A) Every weekend.
3. (B) At the front desk.
4. (C) I'm not sure. But I'll try.
5. (B) Yes, I have a lot to do.

Short Conversations

1. (D) To work overtime.
2. (A) Away from work.
3. (A) 9 a.m.
4. (D) She cannot cook.
5. (C) A travel agent.

Lesson 7

Picture Description

1. (A) The woman is talking on the cellular phone.

2. (D) The man is wearing a hat.

3. (A) They are playing instrument.

4. (B) Several cars are parked on the roadside.

5. (B) There are several railroad buses on the road.

Questions and Responses

1. (B) That sounds good.

2. (A) Put it in the closet.

3. (B) I'm sorry. he's out.

4. (A) Yes, I am

5. (C) From nine to eleven.

Short Conversations

1. (C) A dentist.

2. (B) The company's financial difficulties.

3. (A) A Party.

4. (A) A printer.

5. (C) Some quarters.

Lesson 8

Picture Description

1. (D) There is a car behind the bus.

2. (A) There is a building on the island.

3. (A) The trunk of the limousine is open.

4. (A) There are many people at the restaurant.

5. (B) The people are standing in front of the movie theater.

Questions and Responses

1. (B) I'll do my best.

2. (B) I am sorry. I can't.

3. (A) Yes, I am.

4. (C) Sure, Here you are.

5. (A) Sure, I'll give her the message.

Short Conversations

1. (C) Sunny.

2. (D) Sign up a Korean pitcher.

3. (B) Fireworks.

4. (C) He is on another line.

5. (C) He will read many books on history.

Lesson 9

Picture Description

1. (B) The sign board is by the wall.

2. (C) There are some people in front of the shop.

3. (B) There are several pots.

4. (C) There are many trees behind the cars.

5. (A) The man is carrying baggage.

Questions and Responses

1. (B) On the desk.

2. (B) Yes, I took lessons for two years.

3. (B) I really want to go abroad.

4. (C) I am afraid not.

5. (A) I'll be glad to.

Short Conversations

1. (D) To a ski resort.

2. (C) The machine is broken.

3. (D) He is sick.

4. (C) He wants to rent an apartment.

5. (D) The airline issued too many tickets.